D1230976

LIVING HOMES

SUZI MOORE McGREGOR AND NORA BURBA TRULSSON

LIVING HOMES

PHOTOGRAPHS BY TERRENCE MOORE

SUSTAINABLE ARCHITECTURE AND DESIGN

CHRONICLE BOOKS

SAN FRANCISCO

This book is dedicated to Fran Sneller, Brady and Morgan Barnes, and Jamie McGregor for all their help and for enduring two years with an amplified type-A personality; to Anjelica, Natalia, and Jorgen Trulsson; and to the memory of Lois and Leeland Tenney.

First Chronicle Books LLC paperback edition, published in 2008.

Copyright © 2001 Nora Burba Trulsson and Suzi Moore McGregor. Photographs copyright © 2001 Terrence Moore. All rights reserved. No part of this book may be reproduced in any form without written permission from the publisher.

ISBN: 978-0-8118-6285-1

The Library of Congress has catalogued the previous edition under LCCN: 2001277400.

Manufactured in China

Designed by Chen Design Associates

10 9 8 7 6 5 4 3 2 1

Chronicle Books LLC
680 Second Street
San Francisco, California 94107

www.chroniclebooks.com

Illustration credits:
Pages 18-22, 51-52, William F. Tull
Page 37, Elizabeth Wagner
Page 76, Simone Swan
Pages 80-85, 115, 118, Paul Weiner, Design + Building Consultants, Inc.
Page 101, Tom Wuelpern, Rammed Earth Development
Page 122, Jones Studio
Pages 130-135, 145, 150, Arkin/Tilt Architects
Page 142, Suzi Moore McGregor
Page 174, William McDonough + Partners
Page 181, Robert Mehl

TABLE OF CONTENTS

ADOBE

79 CHAPTER TWO

RAMMED EARTH

PREFACE

It was a workshop on straw bale and rammed earth construction that first sparked the idea for this book. Certainly, there had been plenty of seminars, talks, and workshops on these subjects prior to this— but this event marked one of the early glimmers of interest in alternative building materials by the mainstream design community.

It was 1992, and architect Richard Hoffmeister, then an apprentice at Taliesin West, the Frank Lloyd Wright School of Architecture, had organized a weekend-long workshop at the school's Scottsdale, Arizona, locale. The workshop, which also involved City of Scottsdale building officials and representatives from a local utility company, attracted students, builders, and architects who came to learn more about these two building materials. During the course of the weekend, the workshop participants erected a two-hundred-square-foot, load-bearing straw bale shelter and a rammed earth *banco*, or bench.

The workshop's locale proved to be fruitful. As Taliesin West is a major tourist attraction in metro Phoenix, thousands of visitors come through annually to see Wright's desert buildings and to learn about the 640-acre school, community, and architectural office. Word of the straw bale and rammed earth project circulated, and the site was visited by hundreds from around the world, many of whom were design professionals.

By the mid-1990s, other architects and designers were beginning to move beyond traditional building methods and experiment with straw bale, rammed earth, adobe, and other alternatives, seeking to add to their repertoire.

It occurred to us that two schools of thought, two separate disciplines, were meeting and becoming intertwined. On the one hand, there were the proponents of environmentally and socially conscious building methods, for whom the words *green, sustainable*, and *recycled* had long been in their vocabulary. For them, creating a building out of locally available, energy-efficient materials, often with community-spirited labor, was of utmost importance. The actual design of a structure was of lesser importance. On the other hand, there was the design community—architects, builders, interior designers, landscape architects, and others—for whom the look and lines of a building were paramount.

In recent years, however, the design community has come to embrace alternative building methods and materials, and to become more conscious of energy strategies and other environmental considerations. And environmental activists have come to realize that an Earth-friendly structure doesn't have to be a spartan box. This fusion of design and environmental concerns, of substance and style, has spawned a new type of home— good-looking, functional, and appropriate to the site.

We have found twenty-two such residences in states across the West for this book. We chose to categorize them by their wall materials, starting with adobe homes and rammed earth homes, which represent a continuum of mankind's oldest building material— mud. These homes run the gamut architecturally, from traditional, Pueblo Revival styles, based on Native American structures found along the Rio Grande in New Mexico, to extremely contemporary homes that juxtapose steel and glass with earthen walls. Homes made of straw bale, another category, range from small cottages hand-built by owners to those with modern angular forms built with the aid of professional contractors. Along the way, we've also discovered homes constructed with other wall materials, including native stone, recycled polystyrene, and recycled concrete rubble and also designed to be environmentally respon-

sive and responsible. These form the fourth chapter of the book.

There's a movement happening in home building, a trend toward using appropriate materials to construct environmentally sensitive, energy-efficient houses that also display the hallmarks of good design. It's a movement that you can see on the pages of this book. Our hope is that this book will inspire more of these well-designed, thoughtful homes.

Nora Burba Trulsson
Suzi Moore McGregor
Terrence Moore

ON NATURAL DESIGN

By William McDonough, FAIA

IF WE UNDERSTAND THAT DESIGN LEADS TO THE manifestation of human intention, and if what we make with our hands is to be sacred and honor the earth that gives us life, then the things we make must not only rise from the ground but return to it, soil to soil, water to water, so everything received from the earth can be freely given back without causing harm to any living system. This is ecology. This is good design.

If we use the study of architecture to inform this discourse, and we go back in history, we will see that architects are always working with two elements, mass and membrane. We have the walls of Jericho, mass, and we have tents, membranes. Ancient peoples practiced the art and wisdom of building with mass, such as an adobe-walled hut, to anticipate the scope and direction of the sunshine. They knew how thick a wall needed to be to transfer the heat of the day into the winter night, and how thick it had to be to transfer the coolness into the interior in the summer. They worked well with what we call "capacity" in the walls in terms of storage and thermal lags. They worked with resistance, straw, in the roof to protect from heat loss in the winter and to shield the heat gain in summer from the high sun.

These were very sensible buildings within the climate in which they are located.

With respect to membrane, we only have to look at the bedouin tent to find a design that accomplishes five things at once. In the desert, temperatures often exceed 120 degrees Fahrenheit. There is no shade, no air movement. The black bedouin tent, when pitched, creates deep shade that brings one's sensible temperature down to 95 degrees Fahrenheit. The tent has a very coarse weave, which creates a beautifully illuminated interior, having a million light fixtures. Because of the coarse weave and the black surface, the air inside rises and is drawn through the membrane. So now you have a breeze coming in from the outside, and that drops the sensible temperature even lower, down to 90 degrees Fahrenheit. You may wonder what happens when it rains, with those holes in the tent. The fibers swell up and the tent gets tight as a drum. And of course, you can roll it up and take it with you. The modern tent pales by comparison to this astonishingly elegant construct.

Throughout history, we find constant experimentation between mass and membrane. The challenge has always been, on a certain level, how to combine light with mass and air. This experiment displayed itself powerfully in modern architecture, which arrived with the advent of inexpensive glass. It was unfortunate that at the same time the large sheet of glass showed up, the era of cheap energy was ushered in, too. Because of that, architects no longer rely upon the sun for heat or illumination. I have spoken to thousands of architects, and when I ask the question, "How many of you know how to find true south?" I rarely get a raised hand.

Our culture has adopted a design stratagem that essentially says that if brute force or massive amounts of energy don't work, you're not using enough of it. We made glass buildings that are more about buildings than they are about people. We've used this glass ironically. The hope that glass would connect us to the outdoors was completely stultified by making the buildings sealed. We have created stress in people because we are meant to be connected with the outdoors, but instead we are trapped. Indoor air-quality issues are now becoming very serious. People are sensing how horrifying it can be to be trapped indoors, especially with the thousands upon thousands of chemicals being used to make things today. Very few products appear to have been designed for indoor use.

The architect Le Corbusier said in the early part of this century that a house is a machine for living in. He glorified the steamship, the airplane, the grain elevator. Think about it—a house is a machine for living in. An office is a machine for working in. A church is a machine for praying in? This has become a terrifying prospect, because what has happened is that designers are now designing for the machine and not for people. People talk about solar heating a building, but it isn't the building that is asking to be heated, it is the people. We need to listen to biologist John Todd's idea that we need to work with living machines, not machines for living in. The focus should be on people's needs, and we need clean water, safe materials for cradle-to-cradle life cycles, and durability where appropriate. We need to work from current solar income, and respect diversity, both biological and cultural.

There are certain fundamental laws inherent to the natural world that we can use as models and mentors for human designs. *Ecology* comes from the Greek roots *oikos* and *logos*, "household" and "logical discourse." Thus, it is appropriate, if not imperative, for us to discourse about the logic of our Earth household. To do so, we must first look at our planet and the very processes by which it manifests life, because therein lie the logical principles with which we must work. And we must also consider economy in the true sense of the word. Using the Greek words *oikos* and *nomos*, we speak of natural law and how we measure and manage the relationships within this household, working with the principles our discourse has revealed to us. And how do we measure our work under those laws? Does it make sense to measure it by the paper currency that you have in your wallet? Does it make sense to measure it by a grand summarization called GDP? For if we do, we find that the foundering and rupture of the *Exxon Valdez* tanker was a prosperous event because so much money was spent in Prince William Sound during the cleanup. What then are we really measuring? If we have not put natural resources on the asset side of the ledger, then where are they? Does a forest really become more valuable when it is cut down? Do we really prosper when wild salmon are completely removed from a river?

There are three defining characteristics that we can learn from natural design. The first is that everything we have to work with is already here—the stones, the clay, the wood, the water, the air. All materials given to us by nature are constantly returned to the earth, without even the concept of waste as we understand it. Everything is cycled constantly, with all waste equaling food for other living systems.

The second characteristic is that one thing allowing nature to continually cycle itself through life is energy, and this energy comes from outside the system in the form of perpetual solar income. Not only does nature operate on "current income," but it does not mine or extract energy from the past, it does not use its capital reserves, and it does not borrow from the future. It is an extraordinarily complex and effective system for creating and cycling nutrients, so economical that modern methods of manufacturing pale in comparison to the elegance of natural systems of production.

Finally, the characteristic that sustains this complex and effective system of metabolism and creation is biodiversity. What prevents living systems from running down and veering into chaos is a miraculously intricate and symbiotic relationship between millions of organisms, no two of which are alike. What makes it delightful to humans is cultural diversity.

In thinking about this, I reflect upon the commentary of Ralph Waldo Emerson. In the 1830s, when his wife died, he went to Europe on a sailboat and returned in a steamship. He remarked on the return voyage that he missed the "Aeolian connection." If we abstract this, he went over on a solar-powered, recyclable vehicle operated by craftspersons, working in the open air, practicing ancient arts. He returned in a steel rust bucket, spilling oil on the water and smoke into the sky, operated by people in the darkness shoveling coal into the mouths of boilers. Both ships are objects of design. Both are manifestations of our human intentions.

Most of the buildings today are still steamships. When the sun is outside, we sit inside in the dark burning fossil fuels and creating nuclear isotopes, discussing global warming and radioactive threats.

The homes gathered here in this book represent a new sailboat. What I call a boat for Thoreau. The houses were built by craftspeople, practicing ancient and modern arts, incorporating natural and synthetic technology, working in open air, combining solar power with mass, membrane, and transparency. They represent the hope that the human species might use its singular gift of abundant creativity to move from timeful mindlessness toward a timeless mindfulness.

They signal the human intention to create a new design of design itself.

APPROPRIATE TECHNOLOGY

By David Eisenberg, Co-Director
Development Center for Appropriate Technology
Tucson, Arizona

IN THE FALL OF 1995 I WAS FORTUNATE TO BE A PARTICI-pant in the Ecovillages and Sustainable Communities Conference at the Findhorn Foundation, in northern Scotland. Claire Marcus Cooper began her plenary talk there by having the audience of about four hundred people close our eyes and then mentally travel to the most beautiful place we could remember ever being. She then brought us back to the room in which we were sitting and asked how many of us had imagined that they were in a building. About four people raised their hands. If more buildings had the characteristics of the homes in this book, more people might raise their hands when asked such a question.

When looking at the buildings in this book, I don't find myself thinking of them as buildings, or even as houses. I think of them as homes. I'm not sure many of us can readily make the distinction today between house and home, though there are some very important reasons that we should. At a time when life is being redefined as essentially an economic enterprise, and more people seem to actually believe that time is money, we have also seen the concept of home turned into our "largest financial investment." We are likely to make our critical decisions about our dwellings based on the investment aspects of location, surrounding property values, and how long we think we will live there before moving—typically less than ten years in the United States. Houses have become a commodity.

Houses have changed from the place of family, tradition, nurturing, security, and stability to the place in which we store our possessions and much of our personal financial wealth—if we are both savvy about such things and lucky. In the process they have also been transformed from structures built of local materials used in response to local conditions and traditions, by craftspeople who knew their trade well, with the expectation that they would be passed on from generation to generation, to the modern end-product of an economic, industrial, and financial system. There have been very real improvements and benefits from this transformation, but also some valuable things lost, not the least of which are a sense of place, the appropriateness of the materials or designs used, and many of the critical elements that make communities healthy. Much has been written about these things, so I would like to focus on a different aspect of the impact of this shift.

In reading about or even just looking at the beautiful houses in this book, you may notice an internal tension related to this shift in cultural values. Think about building your own house out of the types of materials used for these houses—earth, straw, natural materials—and then think of using wood frame construction, drywall, and stucco. The latter are code-approved materials sold by well-known companies. Yet we can feel and see the difference in quality between hand-troweled plaster over lath and half-inch-thick drywall with two coats of latex paint over a sprayed-on texture. Do we look at cities in Europe where most of the buildings are hundreds of years old, built of nonindustrial materials and still in use, and contemplate that the useful life for most buildings constructed today is well under a hundred years? Can we experience the same profound feelings in our modern buildings that we do in the great cathedrals, or any of the wonders of ancient architecture, even when visiting ruins like those at Chaco Canyon in the south-western United States?

We feel it, but we no longer trust it. Our "culture" now tells us in subtle and powerful ways that anything new, higher-tech, more sophisticated, more uniform, or predictable is superior to the old, simple, handcrafted, natural, or random. That industrial worldview has structured our thinking, our values, our economic systems, and certainly our understanding and expectations about buildings. But in our gut, we know that there is something amiss. We still value highly the handmade, can still recognize the craftsmanship that comes from attention, knowledge, and skill applied by people to their work. This is not to say that industrial processes are not valuable or important. But we are capable of knowing that there is a difference in quality between handmade and mass-produced that doesn't automatically make either superior to the other. Most of us can still feel the difference.

I have an admitted bias in these things. My focus for many years has been on appropriate technology. My favorite definition is technology that ordinary people can appropriate for their own and their community's use and benefit, meaning that they are not dependent on some large infrastructure over which they have no control. I also define appropriate technology as the lowest or simplest level of technology that can be used to do well that which needs be done. Why care about the level of technology that gets used? My interest lies in the modern illusion that we actually know what we are doing and that we are in control of it. The world is an incredibly complex set of interconnected systems, the workings of which are clearly beyond our ability to comprehend. We know very little about what happens as a result of what we do. We can't explain what takes place in the top inch of soil, or how, as Buckminster Fuller pointed out, we transform a peanut butter sandwich into fingernails, bone, eyes, or brain cells. What do I really know about all the things that happened in the process of taking twenty tons of resources and turning them into the four-pound laptop computer on which I am writing this? Most of the consequences of what we do are invisible to us and are therefore unintentional. The higher the level of technology, the higher the level of unintended consequences—the less we are able to know about what actually happens as a result of what we do.

According to the Worldwatch Institute, buildings account for 40 percent of the material resource flows through the global economy and 40 percent of all the energy used. Humans, as a result of mining activity alone, now move more material on the face of Earth than all the world's rivers. Now think about the fact that of the six billion people sharing this planet at the turn of the millennium, only two billion are living and work-ing in the modern industrial buildings that we know in the developed world. Another third are living in earthen structures, adobe, rammed earth, puddled earth, cob, wattle and daub, and so forth. The remaining two bil-lion people are living in other kinds of indigenous, non-industrial buildings, junk buildings made of scavenged materials fashioned into some form of shelter, or, for a couple of hundred million people today, no buildings at all. Is it even remotely possible, within the biophysical limits of this planet, to house the other two-thirds of the population of the world in the resource-intensive—though labor-efficient and profitable—and highly wasteful and polluting way that it is being done for those of us in the developed world?

When we consider what it is that our buildings actually do—all the things that happen in the full life cycle of the building, including what happens to the very real people who spend much of their lives within them—we see that most of it has remained outside our thinking. We would be well advised to adopt some principles about what buildings should and shouldn't do. A good start would be a sort of Hippocratic corollary, a basic principle that buildings should first do no harm.

If we are going to think about the harm a building does, we need to consider the full range of impacts for the whole life cycle of the building, beginning with the acquisition of resources, the transportation of those resources, the processing and manufacture of materials, components, equipment, and so on, and more transportation, and more processing, and more transportation. Next are the impacts of the building where it sits on the land; was it agricultural land or wilderness turned into residential or commercial development? Then there are the impacts of the assembly of all those components into the building itself, all the fasteners, adhesives, and waste. Next we would consider the flow of resources through the building over its useful life for repair, maintenance, remodeling, ventilating, heating, cooling, lighting, and provision of water and wastewater services. Finally, we would need to consider the impacts of the building at the end of its useful life. Can we somehow modify and reuse the building, or can we disassemble it and reuse the parts or recycle them, or can they go back to nature without causing harm? Are they toxic or just so altered that they cannot be used for anything else and have to be disposed of in landfills?

Is it not astounding that there has been so little consideration of these questions when 40 percent of our annual use of planetary wealth is being invested in buildings? I contend that the homes in this book and the efforts around the world to maintain the ancient wisdom of building and to find regenerative rather than destructive ways of building are a critical part of the transition to sustainable building and development. The industrialized methods of building and the westernization of cultures around the world are convincing people to reject their much more sustainable, though sometimes problematic, traditional methods in favor of our far more problematic and far less sustainable ones. When traditional methods are supplemented with appropriate technological and design improvements, the resulting buildings are frequently superior to their newer, more expensive, and higher-impact industrial counterparts.

Books and houses like these, and the larger awareness of these issues that they create, help generate support for the research, testing, and standards development efforts needed for these materials and methods to gain mainstream acceptance in the developed world. This is the only realistic way to reestablish their credibility and reverse their rejection in both developing and developed countries.

When you look at these homes, I hope you will see them as compellingly beautiful, and deeply attractive to your aesthetic tastes. I hope that you also acknowledge the difficulty and expense to which the owners, designers, builders, and others have gone to gain permission to build such structures or use such materials. In the end, I hope you see them as an important vehicle for change, even if their designers, builders, and owners were just pursuing the dream of beautiful and honest places they could call home.

[chapter **1**]

ADOBE

THE ORIGIN OF THE WORD *ADOBE* CAN BE TRACED TO the time of the Egyptian pharaohs. In Coptic, or ancient Egyptian, the word *tobe* means "brick." The Arabs later translated it to *attob*. From there, it made its way across the Strait of Gibraltar into Spain and became *adobe,* or brick made from earth. Today, we use *adobe* to mean the soil that makes the bricks, the bricks themselves, or the houses made from these bricks.

Building with mud bricks began far before the origin of the word *adobe*. The oldest engineered structures were made of adobe bricks. Even today, adobe is one of the world's most popular building materials, in climates and cultures as diverse as the high-elevation resort towns of Colorado's Rocky Mountains to the sparsely populated villages of Africa's searing-hot deserts. In the early Neolithic period, about 7000 B.C., adobe bricks were used to construct one of the world's first cities, Catalhoyuk, in what is now south-central Turkey, a land of freezing winds and snow in the winter and unrelenting heat in the summer. During the height of occupation, more than ten thousand people lived in a labyrinth of freestanding shelters divided by narrow passages. The shelters were close enough that one wall shaded a neigh-

boring wall, thereby achieving a highly insulated architecture. Entrance was through roof openings that also served as smoke holes for cooking and heating fires.

For thousands of years throughout the Middle East and North Africa, many structures in ancient cities—from simple huts to spectacular mosques—were built with adobe bricks. The material was readily available, particularly in arid regions where trees were scarce. The Moors of North Africa most likely introduced adobe-making techniques to the Spaniards when they conquered the Iberian Peninsula in the eighth century. The Spaniards, in turn, took the knowledge with them to the New World, particularly Mexico and what now is the American Southwest. However, by the time Francisco Vásquez de Coronado entered New Mexico's Rio Grande Valley in 1540, he found indigenous peoples so well versed in mud construction that they were building pueblos several stories high.

As native tribes of the Southwest developed agriculturally based societies, their structures became more sophisticated and more permanent. The Hohokam of southern Arizona, Mogollon of central Arizona and New Mexico, and Anasazi of the Four Corners region

each had their distinctive cultures, but built surprisingly sophisticated shelters and villages. They used hand-formed, sun-dried adobe bricks and also built structures with coursed adobe, in which a stiff mixture of mud blended with stones and shards was applied in layers to create a wall. Some tribes used slabs of rock to construct vast walls mortared with mud and sometimes plastered with the same mixture.

Still other Native Americans chose sites in river valleys. Captain Hernando de Alvarado, leading a party of Spanish explorers to the Rio Grande Valley in 1540, eventually arrived at the present-day site of the Taos Pueblo, considered to be the oldest continually occupied adobe structure in North America. He found two communal, stair-stepped buildings four and five stories high. The roof structures were made by laying logs across the top of walls, then crisscrossing them with reeds and brush and applying layers of mud. Because the pueblo dwellers lacked advanced cutting tools, the ends of the logs pierced through the edges of the walls. Entrances were originally on rooftops, which, as at Catalhoyuk, doubled as smoke holes. Wooden ladders facilitated access, but could be pulled up to defend homes. The women traditionally attended to the annual plastering and repairing of the adobe walls and roof.

Mesa tops were the site of other settlements, such as the Acoma Pueblo in New Mexico, occupied since A.D. 1100. The multistoried villages were built from stone and adobe brick, since both materials were locally available. Long windowless walls on the north shielded the structures from the cold northern winds. On the south, each level was stepped back the depth of one unit, creating roof terraces that were used in warmer months. Common walls provided extra insulation.

As the Spaniards began to settle the Southwest, they brought with them their tools and architectural traditions. They taught the indigenous people to make adobes by pouring a mixture of mud, sand, and straw and other binders into crude wooden forms. Iron tools, the adze and the ax, allowed the logs used as beams for the roof—*vigas* in Spanish—to be shaped into squares. Corbels and other decorative wood trim could also be made. Ceilings were finished by peeling and laying crosspieces such as aspen or cottonwood poles, known as *latillas,* or pieces of cedar might be split and arranged in a herringbone pattern. The roof was built with enough pitch so water would drain into roof spouts, or *canales,* which emptied the water a foot or so away from the adobe walls. The Spanish introduced the corner fireplace. Floors were made of earth, as they were before the arrival of the Spanish.

Larger structures were patterned after the Spanish town plaza, a plan that originated with the Moors, using high windowless exterior walls for defense. Rooms were strung together around an interior courtyard and entered through a gated *zaguán,* or breezeway. Doorways that opened onto the courtyard provided the main source of ventilation and light. The few windows were small and made from sheets of mica. In smaller homes, rooms were arrayed in a line, L-shape, or horseshoe. A portal, or covered walkway, connecting the rooms doubled as an exterior hall. Several families sometimes banded together and built their homes around a central courtyard, or *placita,* achieving the same result as their wealthy neighbors.

Adobe architecture did not arrive in California until the 1700s, when the Spanish began establishing a chain of missions throughout the region. The Mission Style was greatly influenced by Roman and Moorish architecture with arches, open courtyards, and colonnades. After several missions experienced damage or total destruction during earthquakes, wall thicknesses were increased and in some cases buttresses were added. *Presidios,* or forts, built to protect the missions from the native populations, were made from adobe blocks. Resembling the Spanish hacienda, they contained military quarters, supply stores, stables, and maybe a chapel, arranged in a square with defendable entrances. Towns with adobe structures were established near presidios or ports, such as Santa Barbara.

Architectural styles remained fairly stable until several major events changed the look of the West. In 1821, the Santa Fe Trail opened the door for trade between New Mexico—then a part of Mexico—and the United States. With the trail, came an influx of Anglos and wagon loads of building supplies. By the 1840s, New Mexico and Arizona had become territories of the United States, encouraging more settlement by Anglos. By 1848, Santa Fe had its own sawmill. The settlers started imposing what they considered a more "civilized" style on the Southwest's adobe buildings. An early Territorial Style developed with several notable features, including capping the adobe parapet with fired brick or wood and creating walls with sharp-edged corners. Glass became available, and windows were often framed in wood pediments. Flat-roofed adobe homes opened outward onto porches with white columns and porches reminiscent of Greek Revival homes in the East.

With the coming of the railroad in 1879 and greater numbers of Anglos, new materials made their way west. In northern New Mexico, settlers favored pitched roofs, often constructed of corrugated tin, which shed rain and snow more effectively than flat roofs. Fired bricks in a wide variety of colors, wood flooring, and wood trim in ornate patterns all became available. In time, new settlers brought their architecture with them, whether from the Midwest or the East Coast, or from Europe. Victorian bric-a-brac decorated facades of stately old adobes. In new construction, fired brick began to replace adobe. Traditional sun-baked adobe, having become synonymous with poverty, lost its appeal. Many traditional adobe homes received radical facelifts to disguise their ancestry. The West was in danger of losing its architectural identity.

The first rumblings of a Pueblo Revival style came as early as 1905, with architect Mary Colter's Hopi house built at the Grand Canyon. By 1916, Taos and Santa Fe were becoming tourist attractions, and leaders in both locales were concerned that all the new architecture would make their communities look like any other city "back East." Economic survival—the need to attract new tourists—gave birth to strict building codes that encouraged an indigenous architecture reminiscent of the early pueblos. This Pueblo Revival style emphasized the stepped-back facade of the pueblos with rounded corners, flat roofs, and protruding vigas.

Romanticized by journalists in the late 1800s and early 1900s, California's Mission Style was revived. The use of red tile roofs, deep eaves, arches, colonnaded walkways, bell towers, and stuccoed walls characterized what is sometimes also referred to as Spanish Colonial Revival. To a lesser degree, the Territorial Style, with its brick coping and Greek Revival trim, was also revived in the early part of the twentieth century.

Despite the resurgence of these styles, the popularity of adobe architecture went through peaks and valleys, particularly after World War II. But since the 1970s, interest in building environmentally sound and energy-efficient homes has brought renewed focus on adobe, which can be adapted for most climates. Today adobes are no longer hand-formed as they were in the days of Catalhoyuk. But like the Spanish colonists, many owner-builders or contractors still blend soils in a pit at the building site and use wood forms to shape the bricks.

Traditionally, formulas for making adobes were handed down generation to generation. If soils were bad, straw or manure was sometimes mixed in. The type of earth in an area determines if durable adobes can be made without the importation of other soils. Too much clay in the mixture, and the blocks will shrink and crack. Too much sand, and the blocks will crumble and lack strength. Salts in the soil can leach out and become corrosive. Fortunately, soil analysis in the Southwest has become a precise science, and soil-testing laboratories are found in many communities. A primitive method of testing for durable adobes is to half fill a glass with earth from a site, then add water. The heavier particles sink, starting with gravel, then sand and silt. Suspended longest are clay particles. The most desirable composition consists of equal parts of sand and clay. Another test is termed by some builders as the "drop test." A test block is made and

allowed to dry thoroughly—up to two weeks—then is dropped from a height of three feet. If it survives intact, it passes the test.

Many builders and homeowners prefer to purchase adobe bricks from a commercial supplier. At many adobe yards that have sprung up around the West in the last two decades, soils are loaded into the hopper of automated lay-down machines and repetitively extruded into metal forms, spewing out large quantities of adobe bricks in a short amount of time. These adobes can be stabilized with small percentages of asphalt emulsion to make them moisture resistant. Cement added to the adobe block binds to the soil, making it more of a soil-cement block than a stabilized, unfired adobe brick. As for appearance, the difference between the two is a matter of preference. Blocks with asphalt are darker in color. Blocks with cement are lighter in color and more uniform looking than untreated adobes.

The typical adobe wall is built on top of a foundation of concrete block, or stone and mortar, which rises high enough above ground level to eliminate the erosional action of standing water. Tar can be used as a moisture barrier between the concrete block and adobe. A concrete bond beam formed on top of the last course of adobe ties the wall together and supports the roof framing.

In essence, a simple adobe wall acts as a thermal flywheel. Its mass slowly absorbs the heat of the sun during the day, then releases the heat into the interior by night. This works well in moderate and hot climates. Builders of energy-efficient homes often augment these thermal qualities with insulation, particularly in cold climates. Double-adobe walls provide extra mass, and the space in between accommodates additional insulation and wiring. In some cases, builders may add insulation to exterior or interior walls before plastering or stuccoing.

Some adobe walls are left exposed, and deep overhangs protect them from moisture. Most homeowners, though, opt to plaster or stucco the exterior walls. Because the adobe blocks can be easily chipped or sculpted, home designs, particularly the popular Pueblo Revival, often feature gently curving walls.

Although adobe has an ancient history as an efficient and effective building material, it is often chosen by today's builders for aesthetic and emotional reasons. It is considered romantic and sculptural, and it lends itself to a variety of architectural styles. Ironically, in many communities, adobe has gone from being the building material of the poor to that of the well-heeled. Depending on the locale, high labor and transportation costs, lack of competition, and stringent zoning regulations have considerably raised the price of building an adobe home.

Whether they mix the adobe themselves and have a shoestring budget, or create a magnificent dream house, owners of adobe homes will likely never want to live in another kind of house.

GREENLEE RESIDENCE

Cortez, Colorado

Outside Cortez, in the southwestern corner of Colorado, strong winds swirl around stands of piñon pine and juniper. Barely visible to the south is a major Four Corners landmark, Ship Rock, which the Navajo call Tse'Bit'Ai, meaning "rock with wings." To the southeast lies Sleeping Ute Mountain and scattered villages inhabited by Ute tribal members. To the east is Mesa Verde.

Storms in this area roll in suddenly, ravaging the land and eroding the soil. A clear, hot summer day can change within minutes to a sky filled with moisture-laden dark clouds. Temperatures plummet and lightening illuminates the sky while thunder rattles windowpanes and torrential rains slash through the air. Just as suddenly, the winds cease and the sun breaks through the clouds. Winter storms often approach with the same ferocity as summer storms, except the winds are colder, last longer, and bring the possibility of sleet and snow.

When Diane and Bob Greenlee purchased thirty-five acres of land here, they decided to build a vacation home drawing on indigenous adobe traditions that responded to availability of materials and extreme temperature swings. The Greenlees chose a Pueblo Revival style, characterized by a flat roof, vigas protruding beyond the exterior walls, a stepped or terraced elevation, and rounded corners.

The Pueblo Revival adobe home has a wrap-around portal that functions as an outdoor room during warm weather. South-facing doors and windows add daylighting and heat during winter months.

Right: Nestled between piñon and juniper trees, the adobe home is carefully situated to take advantage of the sun and spectacular views. In the distance is Mesa Verde National Park, a major archaeological site where numerous ancestral Puebloan ruins have been discovered.

For many years the Greenlees have participated in archaeological digs. Bob Greenlee, the former mayor of Boulder and a city council member, is an active board member at Crow Canyon, a nearby archaeological center. Since Diane Greenlee had been involved in the design process of several houses they had lived in, building a retreat in southwestern Colorado, an area rich in ancient history, held great appeal.

After purchasing land from a fellow Crow Canyon board member, they sought a local builder who would understand their ideas. Through word of mouth, the Greenlees heard about a contractor, Todd Swanson, known for his creative craftsmanship and expertise in adobe.

Within their parcel, the Greenlees chose a building site surrounded by boulders, piñon and juniper trees, sage, and other high-desert scrub, which created natural rock gardens. In the spring, the colors of wildflowers add to the palette of earth tones. Nature, the Greenlees decided, would lead the design process.

Determined to preserve the vegetation, the Greenlees worked closely with Swanson and Boulder architect Bill Sawyers to design a compact, two-story, 1,400-square-foot floor plan. They came up with a one bedroom design that includes an office and a great room. There are two entries to the house, the formal one on the north end of the east wall, and the one everyone uses, through an outdoor portal, or porch, which wraps around the east, south, and west sides of the house. Bob Greenlee regards the portal as his favorite room, where he spends much of the day reading and relaxing. Just inside, the great room, comprising living and dining areas, takes up the southern end of the house. A large square kitchen opens onto the dining area. Access to the master bedroom is through a pair of antique Spanish Colonial doors on the north end of the living area or by way of an outside door on the west side of the portal. Adjacent to the main entry is a stairway to the upstairs office and bathroom. The office opens onto a west-facing balcony, giving the Greenlees a spot to enjoy the end of the day.

Swanson started building the Greenlees' home by making adobe bricks from the soil in an old pasture next to the house site. First, he scraped off the topsoil and put it aside for later use, when the land would be reseeded. Crusher fines, the very fine waste material from a gravel pit, were dumped on top of the disturbed area. A six-foot-wide tiller, hauled behind a tractor, blended the earth and fines together. A garden hose was used to add water. Swanson tested the mix for the

Opposite: A corner fireplace heats the great room except on rare winter days when backup radiant floor heat is necessary. The hearth is made from buff sandstone. Native American art, antiques, and rustic furniture tie the house to the region's historic roots.

correct plasticity by balling it up in his hands. When the mix felt right, neither too wet nor too dry, he loaded the soil into a hopper, where it was gravity-fed into a press mold, which produced adobe blocks, ten by four by fourteen inches, that tested at a structurally sound three thousand pounds per square inch. During the block-making process, the adobes required so little moisture that the bricks could be used within twenty-four hours, as opposed to conventional adobe blocks, which can require weeks to cure, depending on the weather. The pasture was later recontoured and reseeded. Today it is impossible to tell that the land underwent excavation.

To build a twenty-foot-high adobe wall for the great room, Todd started with a thirty-inch-thick base of adobes and then tapered the walls as they went up, using concrete mortar for the joints. Wall corners were rounded to achieve the Pueblo Revival look the Greenlees desired, then stuccoed.

Inside the house, Pueblo Revival architectural details abound. A corner beehive fireplace warms the great room. Close to the high ceiling line is a bank of small clerestory windows that bathe the upper half of the room with rich, warm light. Large vigas span the width of the room, and those that extend beyond the exterior walls

are fitted with metal flashings to protect the wood from weathering. The *latillas*—aspen poles from a local source—were peeled at the building site. Upstairs, in the office, a *banco,* or built-in masonry bench, extends the room's fireplace hearth into a seating area. The Greenlees' spacious kitchen has a festive ambience, thanks to the brick red cabinetry and teal window sashes.

With the help of Rick Watson, an expert plasterer, the thick interior walls look as if they have stood for centuries. Watson mixed the plaster with pure pigments, including iron oxide, and troweled the surface to a smooth finish, giving the walls a soft uneven tint. Irregular openings between rooms, along with the rounded corners, add character to the walls. Diane Greenlee opted for high-fired Italian floor tiles that resemble low-fired Mexican tiles, but are more durable and easier to maintain.

The Greenlees were interested in more than just a nice-looking house. They wanted one that responded to the environment, and they carefully planned details to accomplish this goal. An insulative skin of polystyrene was added to the exterior walls before the stucco was applied, to help stabilize the interior space during extreme temperature fluctuations. The roof of the portal

Opposite, clockwise from top left:

A bank of clerestory windows adds daylighting to the upper portion of the great room. The latillas are peeled aspen poles from a local source.

An old Pueblo mask is displayed in a niche in the stairway wall.

Taos artist Robert Lavadie carved the corbels and beam in the great room. Bob Greenlee painted the designs with oil stains.

On the exterior of the great room, a line of clerestory windows highlighted by teal trim add interest to the adobe-colored walls.

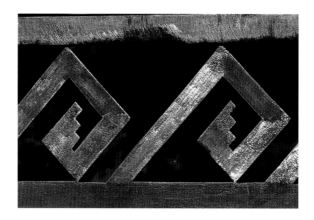

protects the house from the strong summer sun, but allows the winter sun to enter though the glass doors and windows and heat the interior. The corner fireplace in the living area of the great room throws enough heat to keep the Greenlees comfortable on most winter days. The master bedroom fireplace—inspired by one in Georgia O'Keeffe's home in Abiquiu, New Mexico—and one in the upstairs office keep the rest of the house warm. In the winter months, the Greenlees sometimes use the radiant floor heat, which is a shared system with the domestic hot water. In summer, rooms are cooled by opening windows and turning on ceiling fans. The kitchen skylight opens to vent out hot air. Shutters also help keep the hot summer sun at bay.

When choosing furnishings and accessories, the Greenlees focused on the area's history. Antique pieces are mixed with rustic furniture, Navajo rugs, and Native American pottery. In honor of Georgia O'Keeffe's architectural influence, a black-and-white photograph of her hangs next to the master bedroom fireplace. The upstairs office has a desk and computer workstation facing a large picture window that looks out across the southern landscape.

Bob Greenlee fell in love with this part of Colorado the first time he walked the land, but Diane Greenlee wondered about the amount of time they would actually spend at Casa Verde, or Green House, the name they gave their Four Corners retreat. They made careful decisions concerning the design and materials, and how the house would work within the limitations of the land and climate. They also chose a style of architecture and furnishings that have obvious regional connections to the past. Because of the choices they made, the Greenlees spend more and more time at Casa Verde and hope to retire there someday.

Above: The homeowners designed an entry gate for the front garden and commissioned a local welder to fabricate it.

Opposite: A skylight with operable window vents out the hot air, captures cool summer breezes, and brings daylight into the kitchen. Teal window sashes and brick red cabinetry add color to a basically neutral palette.

SMITH RESIDENCE

Tesuque, New Mexico

Set below a ridge,
the Smith residence
has the hallmarks of
the Territorial Style
prevalent in northern
New Mexico: a pitched
metal roof, double-
hung windows, shutters,
and a portal.

Just miles from Santa Fe, New Mexico, a road winds north past the last vestiges of the condominium developments that line the fringes of town, alongside pine-dotted mountains and down into a pastoral valley, marked by small farms, fields, horse trails, and homes tucked beneath huge cottonwood trees.

The Tewa-speaking people inhabited this valley for hundreds of years before the arrival of the Spanish in the late sixteenth century. The native peoples built their mud-walled community, now known as the Tesuque Pueblo, to take advantage of the valley's plentiful water and rich soil. As history has it, the uprising of the Indian people against Spanish oppression—the Pueblo Revolt of 1680—began here with the murder of two Spaniards by the Puebloans. The Spaniards prevailed and eventually established the nearby village of Tesuque in 1740.

Since Spanish times, Tesuque, which means "the place where the cottonwoods grow" in the Tewa language, has always been the country cousin of the more worldly Santa Fe—and therein lies its appeal. Even the ancient Tesuque Pueblo has resisted government modernization, and old mud homes, some rising two stories, remain intact after centuries. In the last few decades, though, the adjacent village of Tesuque has grown to include artists and woodcarvers; a market and a few small businesses mark the center of town.

It was just this country ambience that attracted Santa Fe interior designer Jane Smith to Tesuque. During her spare time, she had hiked the shady trail that runs along Big Tesuque Creek and dreamed of living in the peaceful valley, away from the stresses of Santa Fe's increased urbanization.

In 1992, Smith found a creekside property on the market. Its owner had lived in a small house there for sixty-nine years—typical for Tesuque, where roots run deep. Situated at the base of a ridge, the three-and-a-half-acre lot was shaded by cottonwoods and filled with productive plum, pear, and apple trees. Smith was captivated, and a deal was struck. She knew instantly the kind of house she wanted to build on the site.

In addition to interior design, Smith's background includes fashion design and a stint running a gallery with the late Santa Fe builder and designer Betty Stewart. Stewart was well known locally in the 1970s and 1980s for her Territorial-Style adobe homes, inspired by the architecture of northern New Mexico from the late nineteenth through the early twentieth centuries. Stewart's architectural designs echoed that

Left: To one side of the house, river-rock walls and steps delineate an outdoor dining area, "paved" in loose straw.

time period's increased Anglo influence on New Mexico's existing Indian and Spanish building styles, characterized by pitched tin roofs, wood-trimmed windows and doors, double-hung windows, and squared-off columns setting off the indigenous adobe walls.

Smith decided to tear down the existing old home and build a Betty Stewart–inspired adobe. To achieve the architectural style, she worked with two Santa Fe designers, architect Elizabeth Wagner, who drew up the home's elevations, and David Gibbons of Thaddeus Design, who created the floor plan.

Gibbons, who had worked with Betty Stewart as a designer, created a simple, workable floor plan for the 1,650-square-foot house. The great room, accommodating the kitchen and living and dining areas, was placed at the front of the house. A partial wall, containing cabinetry, separates the kitchen from the dining and living section of the room, and a north-facing portal, or covered patio, extends the living space into the front garden, which overlooks the creek. A master suite and portal and a guest bedroom and bath were placed at the back of the house; an entry gallery connects public and private sections of the house. A three-car garage, designed to complement the house, was sited at the back of the property.

Wagner detailed the home with Territorial-Style architectural elements. A pitched metal roof marks the great room, and a reverse-pitch metal roof signals the bedroom wing. Double-hung windows with deep, splayed window reveals, shutters, and portals are also traditional elements. Plenty of windows and French doors provide a balanced, cross light for all the rooms.

From the start, Smith knew she wanted to use adobe for the construction of the home's walls. As a design professional herself, she felt that the adobe blocks were the natural building material for the area, in keeping with the region's history, and would provide her with the thick walls and the sculptural quality she desired.

Builder Fritz Staver of F&K Construction, also in Santa Fe, used ten-by-fourteen-by-four-inch adobe blocks, made in a Santa Fe commercial adobe yard. The blocks are considered to be semistabilized; that is, asphalt was added to the water before being mixed with the earth and straw. As opposed to handmade adobe blocks, these semistabilized blocks, common in mainstream residential building, are stamped out in a uniform size and are able to resist moisture if left uncovered by stucco or plaster. They have an "up" and a "down" side. The down side is slightly cupped to accept mortar.

Opposite, clockwise from top left:

Mark Spencer's rose painting hangs prominently in the entry gallery. The owner has dubbed the house "Tesuque Rose," for the many roses that fill the garden.

An old table and a pair of New Mexican–style chairs offer a spot to enjoy breakfast along with views of the front garden.

A half wall separates the dining area from the kitchen. Artist Tom Palmore's longhorn looks out over an antique Mexican table and an antler chandelier.

Old wood beams and mottled plaster add a patina of age to the living room. Antiques combined with contemporary pieces achieve the room's welcoming effect. Radiant heat in the brick flooring warms the interior.

For Smith's house, Staver used concrete mortar and laid the adobe blocks sideways, creating a thick wall. The process, which uses more adobes than conventional block laying, results in what is known in local building parlance as a double-adobe wall. Historically, however, a double-adobe wall often refers to the process of building two walls, side by side, with an air space or insulation in between. The electrical wiring for the house was installed between courses of adobe blocks and also channeled into the earthen walls.

With one inch of plaster on Smith's interior walls, two inches of sprayed-on urethane insulation on exterior walls (a local code requirement), and another inch of stucco on the exterior, Staver created an eighteen-inch-thick wall, estimated to have an insulative factor of R-26 to R-30. Smith wanted the wall thickness to give the house a sense of mass and allow for deep window reveals.

The interior was finished off with old, hand-hewn wood beams, adding interest to the high ceilings of the great room and a sense of rugged intimacy to the lower ceilings of the bedroom wing. Hand-troweled plaster was used to give the interior walls an aged, mottled appearance. Heating comes from radiant-heat brick floors installed throughout the house. Doors and

windows provide the cooling. At close to 6,500 feet in elevation, Tesuque can be snowy and cold in winter, but is rarely hot in summer.

The rustic architecture and mass of the house proved to be a good foil for Smith's eclectic collection of Spanish Colonial, Mexican, and European antiques and contemporary furnishings. In the great room, Smith balanced the drama of the ceiling beams with overscale, comfortable seating, a trunk used as a coffee table, and a Navajo rug to delineate the conversation area. An antler chandelier illuminates the dining table and highlights a painting by a contemporary New Mexican artist. The kitchen's festive style was achieved with green-stained cabinetry, copper countertops, and a tumbled-marble backsplash. A hand-carved headboard, a comfortable leather armchair, and Mexican-style nightstands help create a cozy master bedroom.

Despite the various provenances of Smith's furnishings, art, and accessories, the interior has a definite sense of place. It follows a regional tradition dating back to the days when Anglo settlers first arrived in New Mexico, bringing with them a few treasured "eastern" pieces of furniture, which they mixed with locally made, often more rustic, furnishings.

Green-stained cabinetry and copper countertops give the kitchen a rustic look. The windows overlook the creek that runs through the property.

Though Smith enjoys art, particularly works by local artists, she purposely had the house created with few expanses of walls for paintings. Instead, windows frame views of the surrounding gardens, and French doors encourage frequent trips out to the portals.

Though the property had plenty of mature shade and fruit trees when Smith bought it, she asked Faith Okuma, a Santa Fe landscape architect, to create more formal garden areas closer to the house. Okuma added flower beds, planted aspens, and established a small lawn around three sides of the house. A low wrought-iron fence—an antique from the University of Chicago—separates the garden from the creek bank and from the river-rock drive that leads from the front gate up toward the garage in back. A rock barbecue area is set creekside, across from the house.

A small *acequia,* or canal, was built from the ridge in back toward the creek to handle drainage from rains. Smith had a handcrafted metal grate placed over the *acequia* where it runs directly in front of the home's main entry door. The grate is inscribed with the words *Tesuque Rose,* Smith's name for her house, in honor of the many roses that adorn the garden.

With the building process complete, Smith has been able to enjoy the quiet of Tesuque Rose and watch the seasons unfold outside her window. Most of all, she enjoys unwinding on the portal, listening to the sound of the creek, and watching others as they hike or ride horses along the dirt road in front of her adobe house. Like Smith, they too may have a dream of living in the peaceful solitude that is Tesuque.

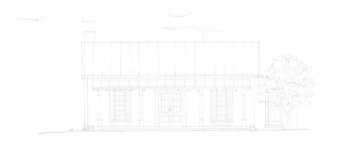

JORGENSEN RESIDENCE

Sugar Loaf Mountain, Colorado

Sugar Loaf Mountain offers a rural alternative to the town life of nearby Boulder, Colorado. Over the years, the area has attracted residents who want to enjoy life in the state's mountain areas and pursue sports and other outdoor activities. Charlotte and Richard Jorgensen appreciate the privacy. It's not easy to find their adobe home at the end of a dirt road that winds up Sugar Loaf Mountain. Switchbacks and forks in the road can be confusing even after a few prior visits.

The property originally belonged to a friend. When the friend moved to England, he let them know the land would be put on the market. The timing was right. The Jorgensens were planning to build an adobe home, and the site proved to be the perfect location. At eight thousand feet in elevation, the land is high enough to support ponderosa pines and aspens. There are also dense stands of scrub oak and meadows filled with wildflowers in the summer.

Charlotte Jorgensen has long been in love with adobe for its soft lines, stability, and closeness to the earth. Richard Jorgensen is a contractor, so together they designed and built the house, planning it carefully to include passive and active energy systems. To achieve the low-profile rustic look the couple desired, they created a one-story floor plan with an east-west axis and built the home into a south-facing hill, which protects and insulates the north—and coldest—side of the house.

The entry doubles as a mudroom, a necessity in Colorado's high country. To the east of the entry is a family room with both kitchen and dining area, a more formal living room, a library, and, finally, a master bedroom suite. Their son Hunter's bedroom and a guest bedroom are on the west end.

The style they chose has elements of Pueblo Revival architecture, including a flat roof with vigas protruding from the exterior walls and rounded corners, but without the multilevel terraces so common in New Mexico. In elevation, the house follows the topography, stepping up or down with the slope of the land, and the earth-colored walls blend in with the hillside, obscuring the distinction between structure and site.

Construction continued for more than nine months before the Jorgensens could occupy the house. When they moved in, the exterior walls still needed plaster and the landscaping had not begun. Three months later the Jorgensens had accomplished both.

Until the time the Jorgensens built their house, homes in the area were traditionally built from logs, wood veneer, wood frame and stucco, or block. Although

The homeowners are collectors of Native American and Southwestern art, which mix compatibly with their furnishings to create a warm, rustic atmosphere. A fine Navajo weaving is used as a rug in the living room. Another vintage Navajo weaving graces the back of a wing chair.

adobe is often built in the high elevations of New Mexico, the building codes in this part of Colorado had no provisions for the material. Since the Jorgensens' house was the first adobe home to pass code in Boulder County, some unusual stipulations were imposed, including a requirement to build with adobe bricks stabilized with asphalt emulsion and to use double-adobe walls with load-bearing posts and beams in between.

To meet these conditions, the Jorgensens bought ten-by-fourteen-inch stabilized adobe bricks from a supplier outside Denver. When they found that the on-site soil was decomposed granite, they had no choice but to import the soil for the mortar as well. It was Charlotte Jorgensen who shoveled this imported soil and sand into a cement mixer. She also helped lay adobe blocks and used an electric planer to peel the old telephone poles that would be used for some of the vigas.

The wood frame cavity between the two adobe walls provided a space for the electrical wiring and insulation. The outside walls were plastered with stabilized adobe mud. Gypsum plaster with a small percentage of a black pigment tints the inside walls a gray-white. The interior walls were given a smooth, burnished finish with the use of a steel trowel.

The Jorgensens' building process wasn't problem-free. When they started digging the foundations, they hit an underground spring. Rather than move the location of the house, Richard Jorgensen came up with a solution that involved piping the water down the hill to the garden, where it bubbles out of a rock with a hole drilled in it.

Some of the massive vigas and *latillas* that span the ceiling were recycled from a demolished building in Larimer Square in Denver. The *latillas* were laid in herringbone pattern. A dealer in Truchas, New Mexico, supplied some of the *latillas* for other rooms. One *latilla* source that Charlotte Jorgensen used for the master bedroom provided saplings that were too green, causing them to shrink and twist as they dried in the ceiling. They were left in place, a reminder that natural materials are not always perfect.

Throughout most of the house, the Jorgensens use an Italian floor tile called Rustica Mexicana, instead of the low-fire Mexican tile often found in Pueblo Revival homes. The Italian tile is more uniform and easier to lay than its Mexican counterpart, but has the same rustic look. The floors in the master suite are made from the hearts of pine.

In the kitchen, a local cabinetmaker used cherry for the cabinetry, complemented by maple countertops. The

Opposite: The kitchen is separated from the rest of the family area by a curved countertop. Glass fronts on some cabinets show off special glasses and dinnerware. The custom copper hood was made by a local metalsmith.

Above, left: A long patio extends the length of the home and beyond, just outside the dining room, at the front of the house. This is where the homeowners spend most of their time during warm months. Hollyhocks, old roses, and other flowering plants thrive against the warm adobe walls, where their growing season is longer than that of plants in areas without supplemental heat gain.

Above, right: A window wall and glass doors in the dining room open up to the lush gardens outside. The south-facing window wall also keeps the room warm during the cold months.

Opposite: The bedroom's east window provides morning light. The corner fireplace is used to augment the heat collected throughout the day from the direct sun pouring in the south window. On rare occasions, radiant floor heat is used in the winter months. The flooring is heart of pine. Fine, white linen and lace cover the bed.

Left: Richard Jorgensen's office is set above the garage, away from the activity of the main house. A building contractor, Jorgensen designed slabs of sandstone and massive poles to separate the office into a work space, a library/ conversation area, a conference room, and a kitchenette and storage area.

Jorgensens commissioned a local company to design a copper hood for the commercial stove. A curved island with a sink and a food preparation area separates the kitchen from the family room. A step-down dining area on the south end of the family room is located next to a window wall overlooking the garden and the forest beyond. The living room and library act as a buffer between the family room and the master bedroom at the far east end of the house. Throughout the house, the Jorgensens used four-panel fir doors. Beehive fireplaces with wrap-around hearths add focal points and warmth to the living room, family room, and master suite.

The Jorgensens carefully planned their house to take advantage of the site and the numerous sunny days. Eighteen solar panels, located behind the house on top of the hill, are used for the hot-water heater and backup radiant floor heating, as well as for the swimming pool and hot tub. The south window walls act as passive collectors of solar radiation and flood the interior with natural light. Skylights can be opened for ventilation while adding light to the northern side of the house, where the walls are against solid earth. Jorgensens selected windows with triple-pane, heat mirror glass that minimizes excessive heat loss or gain.

The Jorgensens' furnishings complement the architec-ture. Old and new Navajo rugs are displayed on walls and floors, and the artwork includes paintings of Southwest-ern landscapes. The furniture is a mix of antiques and comfortable pieces with cotton or leather upholstery. Window coverings in the master bedroom and dining area, simple linen scrim curtains hung on hand-forged iron rods, filter out the harsh midday light.

Charlotte Jorgensen planted expansive gardens, which terrace down a hillside to a meadow below. Herbs were placed close to the front of the house. Hollyhocks, blooming in midsummer, line up against the adobe walls. Peonies, old roses, and other flowering plants are mixed in with ground cover and native flora. Because adobe walls retain heat, Jorgensen noticed that flowers planted near the exterior walls had a longer growing season than those planted away from the house.

The high Colorado mountains suit the Jorgensens, active people who enjoy hiking, skiing, and other activities throughout the year. In summer they spend most of their time moving between house and garden, often eating outside. In winter, they can cross-country ski from their own front yard. The Jorgensens have created a home that works as a center of family activity, as well as an embodiment of their environmental ethos.

Opposite: A handcrafted,
arched entry door was set
into the massive adobe
walls. Because the home
was the first adobe to be
permitted in Boulder
County, the homeowners
had to build double-adobe
walls with a supporting
timber wall in between
for added structure.

Right: A greenhouse spans
the south side of an adobe
barn.

ADOBES DE LA TIERRA

Scottsdale, Arizona

In north Scottsdale, the Sonoran Desert rises in elevation. Enormous granite boulders, rocky hillsides, and deep arroyos mark the topography. The sparse creosote scrub of the lower elevations gives way to a forest of towering saguaro cacti and native mesquites, palo verdes, and ironwoods. The land was once home to the ancient Hohokam people; the ruins of their dwellings and the rings of their fire pits can still be found here. In the late nineteenth century, military wagon trains crossed the region between forts, and cattle and sheep ranchers vied for grazing lands. Miners discovered that the granite rock formations and hillsides also yielded small amounts of gold and, later, gypsum. Until the late 1950s, though, the area was sparsely populated.

In recent decades, the area's population steadily increased as people were drawn to the geography and the desert flora. Many custom homes began to take shape in the desert. By the late 1980s, some of the metro area's most interesting and innovative homes were being built there.

It was here among the boulders and saguaros that artist and architectural designer William Tull chose to build Adobes de la Tierra, a "village" made of his favorite sculpting medium—adobe. The sixteen completed homes hug the undulating desert terrain, and although each home has a distinct architectural style, all showcase Tull's ability to blend building into land.

The Adobes de la Tierra project was the culmination of a decades-old dream and of Tull's second career as an artist and designer. Though his education is in fine art, Tull spent his early years working in New York's advertising scene before moving to Scottsdale to pursue painting full time. Tull and his wife, Jo Ann, an interior designer, became smitten with the historic ambience, and the thick walls and regional appropriateness of adobe construction, when they lived in and remodeled several old adobe homes. At the time, in the 1960s, interest in building with adobe was at an all-time low in metro Phoenix. Local builders had virtually given up on the material after World War II. In 1968, when the Tulls decided to design and build their own adobe home, they discovered that city codes no longer even permitted the material. They wound up building the Pueblo Revival home out of concrete masonry block.

Above: The rounded forms of plastered adobe have become William Tull's favorite sculpting medium.

Opposite: A sculptural corner fireplace warms the entry to an adobe home. Peeled poles make a rustic overhang above the door.

The desert floor was bermed to meet the windows of some residences, creating a close relationship between house and nature. Pink penstemon and orange-blossomed Mexican honeysuckle color the desert landscape.

Dramatically balancing granite boulders typical of the area create a spectacular backdrop for a patio.

The homes in Adobes de la Tierra are nestled into a desert landscape of yellow brittlebush, desert marigolds, barrel cactus, and palo verde trees.

Tull, however, became determined to bring back adobe as a building material. His determination came to fruition when he hooked up with Arizona builder John Mecham, who had grown up in Santa Fe, New Mexico, surrounded by traditional adobe design. Mecham had helped change the building code of Mesa, Arizona, a metro Phoenix community, to once again include adobe as a viable building material. By 1980, Tull and Mecham had done the same for building codes in other Phoenix-area communities, and they began a collaboration that has continued with the Adobes de la Tierra village.

By the time the adobe village project began, Tull had become known as much for his sculptural, adobe custom homes as for his artwork. The first home he designed for the twenty-acre village was a 2,900-square-foot villa for himself and his wife. He took a design risk by using exposed adobe block—a more rustic look than the smoothly plastered homes for which he had become known. The intimate main house features thick walls, a romantic master suite with a fireplace and a claw-foot tub, an overscale fireplace for the living room, and Tull's signature, view-framing windows, shielded from the sun by shutters made from native saguaro ribs. The home also has a freestanding guest house and garage. The two are attached by multilevel, outdoor patios that wrap around the property's boulders. Jo Ann Tull furnished the house with simple, large-scale pieces and antiques that complement the architecture.

Not long after the project's 1989 grand opening, for which they used their own home as a "model," the house was sold, and more homes were commissioned, placed around the village's meandering, horseshoe-shaped drive and tucked into a setting augmented by the designs of Cave Creek landscape architect Phil Hebets, who added more arid-region trees, shrubs, and wildflowers to the native mix.

The ensuing homes reflected a melding of Tull's artistic vision and the needs of the homeowners, many of whom are winter visitors. The homes range in size from about 3,400 to 7,000 square feet, and several have two stories.

An old, Native American pot catches
light from a small, arched window.

Above, left: A large, gilt-framed mirror reflects the pale-hued dining room of a contemporary-style adobe. Ribs from a saguaro cactus were used to make the grate for the air vent, as well as the shutters. Interlocking hand-hewn beams create an interesting ceiling pattern.

Left: A beehive fireplace, a traditional element in adobe homes, warms another home's dining room.

While some of the sixteen residences have contemporary lines, others recall influences from Santa Fe, Spain, and even Morocco. Throughout the homes, Tull has paid attention to details, creating, for example, domed, plastered ceilings in some rooms; others are protected by massive vigas, decked in peeled sapling *latillas*. Fireplaces are used liberally, both indoors and out, ranging from small, welcoming fireplaces placed near front doors to massive brick-lined hearths that one could almost walk into. The adobe has been sculpted to create splayed window reveals and small niches for displaying art or candles. In many homes, antique Mexican doors and gates were selected for their rustic appeal.

The adobe blocks for all the homes were shipped from a commercial adobe yard in Tucson. Tull and Mecham use stabilized adobe blocks sixteen inches long, twelve inches wide, and four inches thick, laid on end, or perpendicularly, to create a sixteen-inch-thick wall. By code, however, the fireplaces were built of concrete masonry blocks.

As adobe walls are known for their thermal mass, as opposed to insulative properties, the homes have additional insulation. The interior walls were framed out and lined with insulation, then covered with rock lath for interior plaster. The exterior walls were stuccoed. Left without insulation, the adobe walls would operate on a thermal flywheel principle, absorbing the exterior heat slowly during the day and releasing it inside by night. In a hot desert climate, this isn't always desirable, particularly during the summer months—hence, the insulation.

Tull and Mecham also used adobe blocks to create Tull's signature serpentine garden walls, which encircle some of the homes, creating protected courtyards, dining patios, and pool areas.

Against the rounded forms of Tull's adobe architecture, homeowners have responded with a variety of interior furnishings. Some of the interiors are modern and clean; others are furnished with antiques, both European and American, and family heirlooms. The interiors look good with a wide array of styles—no particular look alone is appropriate for the adobes. Comfort seems to be the unifying element, and homeowners have placed furnishings so that views can be seen, fireplaces enjoyed, and private nooks relished.

Perhaps Tull's greatest achievement with Adobes de la Tierra is that one still sees the land—the desert—first and the homes second.

Above: Deeply colored wood flooring and doors add depth to a peaceful sitting room in one of the adobe homes.

Opposite, clockwise from top left:

A massive fireplace anchors the living room of a contemporary-style adobe home in the village. The Moorish-influenced archway leads to the bedroom wing. Artwork above the fireplace is by Scottsdale artist Fritz Scholder.

Bleached vigas and peeled sapling latillas add interest to a guest bedroom. The woody ribs from a saguaro cactus were used to make the shutters.

Thick archways flank an entry hall containing antique furnishings and oriental rugs.

WIGGINS-LOGAN RESIDENCE

Longmont, Colorado

Tall, native grasses help screen the home from the rest of the community. The roofline was designed to echo the property's rolling hills. During winter months, a south-facing window wall brings direct light and heat into the home's interior.

Left: Architect Jim Logan and his wife, sculptor Sherry Wiggins, designed a planned community where they also built their own home.

Opposite, clockwise from top left:

All the homeowners in the community participate in planting and caring for a communal garden that produces a variety of vegetables.

In spring and summer, flower gardens liven up the front of the house. Matchstick bamboo shades on the exterior of a south-facing bedroom screen out the harsh light.

A flower garden adds color to the front of the home.

The grassy hills surrounding Longmont, Colorado, stretch out until they merge with the Rocky Mountains. Winds howl across the prairie during the long winter months, when temperatures occasionally dip below zero. Summer temperatures can reach the hundred-degree mark, making it uncomfortable to be outside midday. It was here, in 1983, that architect Jim Logan and his wife Sherry Wiggins, a sculptor, returned to the site of her childhood roots, a defunct 1970s commune started by her parents.

Intrigued with the idea of developing a community where like-minded people could live and raise their families, Logan and Wiggins helped her parents subdivide a 118-acre parcel for a planned unit development, better known as PUD by the county building department. They drew and submitted designs to the county for seven lots with seven homes, leaving 96 acres preserved as open space and communal areas for shared activities determined by a homeowners' association. During the course of the initial planning, the tenants of the existing homes were given an opportunity to purchase their house and lot. Most took advantage of the offer.

After the community planning was in place, Logan and Wiggins decided to build their own home on a five-acre lot next to her parents' house. They sited it on flat grassland with views of hills, ranches, and farms to the north and the front garden and neighboring homes to the south. Logan drew a 2,100-square-foot plan, which included three bedrooms, a large country-style kitchen, a comfortable living area, and an office/studio. Using an east-west axis, he laid out a basic rectangle. A generous entry doubles as a gallery, and to the east, a short hallway leads to the office/studio and master suite. The west portion of the house consists of a kitchen, a living room, and two bedrooms for the couple's children, Dana and Brian. Although the room sizes are of moderate proportions, high ceilings and numerous window openings add to the overall sense of space.

Wanting to blend the home into its surroundings, Logan and Wiggins utilized a curving roofline to mimic the slopes of the surrounding hills. Their interest in trying two types of earthen architecture led to the use of double adobe for the exterior walls and rammed earth for the interior partition walls. This combination would also boost the amount of thermal mass in the house and enhance the soundproofing between rooms.

Logan, originally a contractor, prefers materials that are low maintenance and age gracefully, improving with time.

He created the double-adobe exterior walls by essentially building a wall within a wall, using adobe bricks trucked in from a source in New Mexico. A twelve-inch air space was filled with cellulose for insulation. A poured-concrete bond beam with reinforced steel caps the final course of adobe and ties the walls together. The bond beam also functions as door and window lintels. The concrete is not hidden by plaster or other materials, but used as a design element in the house. The interior rammed earth walls were built by pouring and tamping moist earth into concrete forms, then allowing them to set up before removing and resetting the forms to build the next level. The interior wall plaster was mixed with black sand found in a nearby wash and then left unpainted.

Galvanized sheet metal covers exterior doors. For the roofing, Logan decided on a corrugated sheet metal insulated with a foot of cellulose. Sheet metal is a highly reflective surface that has a long life span and needs little upkeep. Windowsills are flashed with steel, as is an exterior drip edge between the foundation and the first course of adobe. Logan chose steel because of its durability and the dark patina it acquires with age.

Logan and Wiggins wanted the kitchen to be the social hub. With this in mind, they designed a room large enough for a refectory-style table that can seat eight. The south window wall, which stretches across the kitchen, floods the interior with light and opens the house to the community. Halogen lights are strung on a cable above the countertops. Logan hired a local craftsman to make the kitchen cabinets out of Colorado pine.

Colorado spruce was used for the flooring and paneling throughout the house. Sheet metal, chosen to cover the ceiling in the kitchen and living room, was treated with vinegar to give it a matte finish. The master bedroom is bathed in light from windows on the east and north. German-style windows on the north, which crank inward, frame views of the hills and the mountains beyond. Clerestory windows on the south add light and warmth.

Logan did a number of things to make the house energy efficient. A major strategy was to orient the house to maximize solar gain from large expanses of south-facing windows. A backup system of radiant floor heat ensures comfort even on the coldest days. Solar panels provide hot water for the radiant floor heat and on-demand hot-water heater. Logan concealed the solar panels on the roof by placing them next to the skylights and flush with the roofline. On the north side, windows filled with argon gas help insulate the house.

Above: Furnishings in the conversation area of the living room are of natural materials such as cotton duck and wicker. Noguchi lamps add soft lighting.

Opposite: The kitchen, the social hub of the home, is heated in winter by a passive solar window wall. High windows open in warm months to vent out hot air. Low windows let in cool summer breezes.

Furnishings in the master bedroom are minimal, letting the natural woods be the dominant feature. Deep windowsills can be used as a display or sitting area. An exposed concrete bond beam that doubles as a lintel spans the German-style windows.

Concerned about toxins from paints and stains, Logan and Wiggins researched and experimented with different products. For some wood finishes, they chose milk-based paints mixed with natural pigments. Hand-rubbed organic mineral pigments are used on some interior doors. Other inside doors and wood trim were finished with natural dyes, such as indigo from the indigo plant and cochineal from ground-up cactus beetles. Tung oil seals and enriches the spruce floors.

Against the rich wood backdrops and finely plastered walls, Logan and Wiggins display their artwork, a combination of paintings and large sculpture. Continuing the creation of a healthy house, Wiggins chose natural fabrics woven from cotton for most of the upholstered pieces. Using minimal furnishings, the couple let the architecture and views remain the focus.

Logan and Wiggin's dream has come to fruition. Since they developed the land, the members of the home-owners' association have planted a communal vegetable garden, built a park with swings, a picnic table, and a volley-ball court, erected a communal coop to house chickens that provide fresh eggs, and worked on various other improvements for the benefit of all. There are buildings for meetings, storage, and guests. Community members share responsibilities such as cleaning irrigation ditches and the chicken coop and maintaining the park.

The couple did a lot of experimenting and admit there were some mistakes, but that building their own house was a learning and growing process for future homes. For now, though, the rewards are plentiful. From their kitchen window, Logan and Wiggins can see cats stalking field mice and dogs lounging in the sun. The voices of people are not far off. They need only step outside their home to enter the community they helped to put together.

Local spruce was used for the flooring, closets, and paneling. The wood is sealed with a natural tung oil finish. In the entry, a sculptor pays homage to a onetime grasshopper infestation. Cut flowers are from the garden.

BILLINGS-FERGUSON RESIDENCE

Norwood, Colorado

Susan Billings and Duncan Ferguson's home, set into a slope among piñon and juniper, looks out over canyons to distant mountain ranges. The couple's home is just outside Norwood, a small town in western Colorado, sixty-five miles from the nearest traffic light. Views to the west include Paradox and Disappointment valleys and the La Sal mountain range in Utah. Although this is not high mountain terrain, winter storms can still be ferocious, leaving behind a foot of snow and arctic temperatures. Summers are generally hot and dry, with rainstorms coming in fast and leaving just as quickly. Since moving here, the couple and their two children have come to understand the kind of commitment it takes to live the "simple life."

Originally from Boulder, Colorado, the family decided to relocate here when Duncan Ferguson returned home after working on a film in the Telluride community, not far from Norwood. He fell in love with the landscape on this side of the Rockies and found a thirty-five-acre parcel of land suitable for building.

Ferguson and Billings asked friend and architect Jim Logan, of Longmont, Colorado, to help design a simple, affordable adobe home with its own source of energy. Logan is known for his sensitive approach to architecture, designing passive and active systems for

Opposite: The back of the home is partially bermed into the hill. The front faces the La Sal Mountains. The xeriscape gardens require little, if any, additional water.

Right: The kitchen cabinetry is handcrafted from a recycled warehouse beam. A built-in sitting area multiplies the number of people that the space can accommodate. Matchstick shades help filter out the setting sun.

heat and electricity, using natural materials such as adobe and regional woods that are not endangered, and calculating what natural resources were spent in order to arrive at the final product. Before Logan started drawing the plans, he spent time walking the land, camping on the future house site, noting the direction of the breezes and where the sun would rise and set.

Logan then drew an L-shaped plan made up of two separate structures connected by a wall. He sited the 2,200-square-foot compound at the end of a long, narrow dirt track behind a low hill, screening the house from the main road. The main entry, a great room, a kitchen, and two children's bedrooms—each with a loft—are in one building, and a master bedroom and guest quarters are in the other. The space between the two serves as a patio.

In elevation, the contemporary home's most striking feature is a shed roof, angled to match the slope of an adjacent hillside, making a strong connection between house and land. By using simple lines and basic materials, including adobe, corrugated sheet metal, and wood, Logan has created a distinctive architectural statement, somewhat reminiscent of the old miners' buildings found in the area. The exterior colors blend in with the landscape, except for the lively addition of turquoise

wood trim around the entry door.

The Ferguson-Billings home was the first adobe to be permitted in their county. Previously, most homes were built with conventional materials such as concrete block and wood frame with stucco. To comply with county requirements, the adobe bricks were not made on-site, but trucked in from Whitewater, Colorado, sixty miles away, where the blocks were engineered by a soil specialist and certified to meet rigid county standards. Other requirements for the building permit included using double-adobe walls and stabilizing the first eighteen inches of block, from the ground up, with asphalt emulsion.

Acting as his own contractor, Duncan Ferguson worked closely with local building inspectors and craftsmen, learning as he went along. To keep walls from cracking and shifting apart due to any settling of the earth, Ferguson tied the walls together by forming a concrete bond beam on top of the final course of adobe. The exterior walls were finished with an adobe plaster made from clay, lime, and sand, which would allow the walls to breathe, letting any moisture trapped within to evaporate. An adobe mud plaster was used on the inside walls. Ferguson also added a foundation border of bluff sandstone and mortar to protect the first eighteen inches of adobe from snowfall.

Above, left to right:

On the south patio, the homeowners created a shaded area with poles and cotton canvas. Matchstick bamboo hung from the framework filters the intense sun from the south and west.

The homeowners spend most of the warm months relaxing on the south patio.

The south patio table serves as a shady spot, where fresh chiles are set out to ripen.

Opposite: The south patio has spectacular views of the surrounding countryside. Thick stands of rabbitbrush, sage, pinon, and juniper cover the hills and mesa tops.

The winter sun pours in and heats the concrete floors and adobe walls. In the living area, where furnishings are simple, woven textiles contrast with the natural-colored adobe walls. High, east windows are left open in the summer to vent hot air.

Metal flashings were put between the concrete bond beam and roof framing. The roof is made with two-by-twelves, insulation, plywood, and corrugated sheet metal. Maintenance of the walls and roof is a yearly family project that extends the life of the structure. Any cracks in the plaster are repaired, and roof screws are checked and tightened.

An informal path leads from the parking area to the front of the house. Surrounding the front entry is a veneer of corrugated sheet metal whose reflective surface deflects the sun's intense afternoon rays. The smooth, shiny surface contrasts effectively with the turquoise wood trim outlining a handcrafted front door and the adobe walls.

Inside, a south-facing window wall floods the great room and kitchen with light. French doors set into the wall provide a direct link to the outdoors, where the family spends a great deal of time. The entry, detailed with a wood-clad ceiling and wood paneling, is further enlivened with blue-stained closet doors. Natural-colored, scored concrete floors were used throughout the house. Logan kept the high side of the sloping roofline over the living area of the great room. The low side is over the kitchen and dining area. Logan designed the kitchen with a surprising combination of textures and materials, mixing recycled fir beams for the

countertops with new corrugated sheet metal. Generous window openings provide light and ventilation in the children's bedrooms. In the other building, an open and airy master suite has an expansive window wall that captures the winter sun. The guest bedroom, tucked behind the master suite, opens onto the patio.

Ferguson and Billings worked with Logan to produce an energy-efficient, well-insulated house that is off the grid. Photovoltaic cells located behind the house convert sunlight into energy for electricity. The refrigerator is solar powered, and propane is used as a backup system for the radiant floor heat, a gas stove, and an on-demand hot-water heater. Ferguson put the plumbing and electric wiring inside the four-inch void between the two exterior adobe walls, filling the void with blown cellulose. The wall's twenty-four inches of mass are enough to help keep the interior warm in winter and cool in summer. The corrugated metal roof not only reflects heat from the sun, but also captures the rainwater and snowmelt into a gutter, which drains into one of two underground cisterns. The water is used for irrigation.

Temperature variations in the Norwood area can be dramatic, often reaching one hundred degrees Fahrenheit in the summer and minus twenty-five degrees Fahrenheit

in the winter. Staying warm or cool can be challenging. In winter, concrete floors absorb heat from the sun shining through the southern windows. During cold nights, a woodstove in the main living area augments the passive system. A bank of high operable windows on the east side of the great room is left open in summer to vent out the hot air. On the west end, a bank of windows above the kitchen counter helps heat the house at the end of the day during the cooler months. A bamboo shade filters out the hot summer sun. Outside overhangs also cut the amount of glare on this side of the house.

The home's informal furnishings and rustic decorative pieces create a comfortable environment to spend time and enjoy the views. Large potted cacti and other plants scattered throughout the house help soften the interior.

Susan Billings planted a xeriscape garden, including sage, thyme, lavender, and rabbitbrush, that blends well with the native plants. Seating areas for outdoor dining and conversation are tucked into the patio created between the home's two wings.

The spectacular sunsets in this part of the world light up the sky with a wide range of colors. Even when the Billings-Ferguson family is inside, they feel a strong connection to the landscape beyond their glass walls.

Opposite: The master suite, located in a separate structure from the main house, gives the homeowners privacy. Massive double-adobe walls and careful siting keep the interior temperature fairly stable.

Above, left: Masks from Africa and other artifacts and artwork, collected from the owner's various excursions, decorate the interior walls.

Above, right: A cairn stacked by the homeowners adds interest to the entrance of the house.

SWAN RESIDENCE

Presidio, Texas

Set on top of a mesa, the house is surrounded by creosote, ocotillo, and other native plants.

In West Texas, where the Rio Grande marks the division between Mexico and the United States, the Chihuahuan Desert supports thick stands of ocotillo interspersed with low-growing prickly pear and yucca. Dry riverbeds and washes cut through valleys, which are in sharp contrast to the boulder-strewn hillsides and mountains.

Around Big Bend National Park, the land has always been sparsely populated, first by early Native Americans and later by a handful of miners, ranchers, and farmers. During the past few decades, the area hasn't changed much, possibly because of the climate. Temperatures in the summer can be some of the highest in the nation, averaging 105 degrees Fahrenheit in July. Early in the century, people insulated themselves from the hot sun by building thick-walled homes made from unfired adobe bricks. Today, most Texans in this part of the state build their homes from concrete block and frame with stucco— that is, until Simone Swan moved to the outskirts of Presidio, Texas, and demonstrated a different way to think about housing.

Swan, a publicist for *Fortune* magazine in the early 1960s, opened her own public relations firm in the mid-1960s, specializing in the arts. By 1972 Swan was appointed executive vice president of the Menil Foundation, a philanthropic organization involved in art, architecture, and politics. That was the year she had a life change that started at a Paris dinner party.

That evening, a friend suggested she read *Architecture for the Poor* by Egyptian architect Hassan Fathy. She did, and was so moved by his vision that she wrote the architect of her desire to go to Egypt and work with him. He responded favorably to her request, and Swan flew several times to Egypt, where she visited his projects, helped him with translations, and aided in the creation of an institute for appropriate technology involved in educating people about vernacular housing for low-income families.

Fathy passionately believed in better housing for the poor by making use of native materials, such as earth, sculpted into traditional homes, opposed to "boxes" made from concrete. He understood that such housing would instill pride and give inspiration to the occupants. Egypt has little usable wood for roofing timbers, so Fathy came up with an alternative. He hired craftsmen with knowledge of traditional construction techniques to teach Egypt's poor the ancient art of building vaults, arches, and domes from earth, thereby enabling the people to construct their own homes,

Above: Adobe lends itself to strong walls and rooflines.

Opposite: Peeled vigas span the width of the gallery space. Single-pane French doors line up on the north and south, as well as on the east and west where they lead into the front and rear courtyards. Small clerestory windows on the east wall help illuminate the long space. Five coats of spirits of turpentine and linseed oil were used to seal the mud floor. A sculpture by Arden Scott hangs from the ceiling.

steeped in the rich architectural history of the Middle East and North Africa.

When Swan left Egypt for the final time, she took with her the enthusiasm and knowledge of her mentor. In 1989, Fathy passed away, leaving behind his protégée Swan, who by this time was determined to carry on his ideas.

Some years later while visiting Big Bend National Park, Swan happened on the town of Presidio where historic Fort Leaton, originally an adobe trading post built by Ben Leaton in 1848, was undergoing restoration by the Texas Park Service. The project interested Swan, and she volunteered her time and energy. The job included toting a bucket of mud and a trowel, and served as Swan's introduction to a region where she would later live and carry on Fathy's work.

By 1995, Swan established the Swan Group, a company specializing in low-cost housing built with unfired adobe bricks. Maria Jesusita Jimenez, a local woman, was hired as project manager to supervise construction. Their first project was a prototype house across the border in Mexico for builder Daniel Rodriguez Camacho, a resident of Ojinaga. In a pit at the building site, Camacho mixed mud for his adobes, which he used in the construction of the walls, vaults, and a dome and for mortar and plaster.

The final cost of his L-shaped home came in at eleven dollars per square foot, creating a local interest in adobe architecture. Since finishing his home, Camacho has opened up his own adobe yard to supply the growing demand.

Unable to raise funding for more low-income housing after finishing the Camacho home, the Swan Group experienced a lull. Instead of disbanding the group, Swan decided to build her own home on 432 acres she had purchased on top of a mesa. The site she chose for her house on the property takes advantage of the dramatic views of Chinatic Peak to the north and the Rio Grande to the south, with the Sierra Rica Mountains looming from behind. The land is flat and rocky, with low-growing native plants such as creosote bush mixed in with tall spindly ocotillo. Littered on the ground among the small rocks are the fine, sharp-edged agate flakes chipped off by ancient flint knappers.

The home evolved from Swan's previous experiences with Fathy. She designed the one-story main house in an H-shaped plan. One side of the H contains two bedrooms, each with its own bath. The other has a living space and a kitchen. A long gallery connects the private and public sides. Swan also designed separate guest quarters, making the total living space 1,600 square feet.

Above: In summer, Presidio is one of the hottest areas in the United States. The homeowner limited the number of wall openings exposed to harsh sunlight. The exterior walls are plastered with a breathable lime-and-sand mixture that allows any trapped moisture to escape.

Opposite: French doors lead from the bedroom to the front courtyard. Muslin curtains can be closed for privacy and for muted light during the day. Minimal furnishings allow the architecture to be the focus.

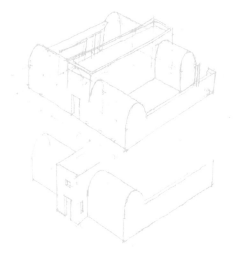

Below: views from the top of the gallery roof look out across the mesa to the distant mountain ranges. This is the homeowner's favorite place to view the stars.

Working with a style reminiscent of historic Egyptian and Iranian architecture, Swan used long, high adobe walls to support the four vaulted-ceiling rooms of the main house. A flat roof marks the gallery space. Off the north wall of the main house is an open carport that uses a wood frame roof system covered with palm fronds to keep the rain out, an idea rooted in Mexican architecture.

Due to poor soil quality, Swan needed to import soils for the traditional adobe bricks that she and her crew mixed and poured into wooden forms. Manure was added to the adobe mixture for viscosity. The adobes were used not only for wall construction, but for the vaults and dome as well. Foundation walls were formed higher than ground level with large rocks and concrete, then coated with tar as a moisture barrier before starting the first course of adobe. A coating of lime-and-sand plaster covers the twenty-inch-thick adobe walls. Swan chose to leave the inside of the vaulted ceilings exposed, which contrasts with the smooth plaster of the interior walls.

Four small clerestory windows help light the gallery. A pair of French doors at each end of the gallery are often left open to help circulate air. Screen doors were added to keep the insects at bay. Window openings in other parts of the house are small to minimize heat loss and gain. Except for the gallery, Swan installed low-fire clay floor tiles from Mexico, known as *saltillos*, which complement the thick adobe walls. The gallery has a poured mud floor composed of the same soil mixture as the adobe bricks, which was then troweled to a smooth finish. Five coats of spirits of turpentine and linseed oil seal the floor.

Swan has also addressed other energy and environmental concerns. A solar refrigerator, a pump for the well, and lights are run off twelve small photovoltaic panels discreetly hidden near a storage building. Heating is not a problem in Presidio.

Against the strength of the architecture, Swan chose to leave the furnishings minimal, almost monastic, with just a bed and table stacked with books in each of the bedrooms. The living room has become more of an office, with long tables, more books, and a few chairs. A functional kitchen has handmade wood cabinets and counter space for food preparation.

Swan planted a regional selection of native cacti near the home's exterior walls. Inside the high courtyard walls, where the land was disturbed by construction, Swan is laying out a more formal garden. Large clay pots hold bougainvillea, and a low, bubbling fountain serves as the courtyard's central focus.

A wooden stairway against the outside entry wall leads to the top of the flat-roofed gallery space, which Swan calls her viewing room. The clarity of the constellations can be dramatic, lighting up the sky. But Swan is not satisfied, and will not be, until she finds funding for the housing project she and Hassan Fathy had envisioned. Lately, more interest in the endeavor has led to several prospects, which is uplifting to Swan, who believes, "All people deserve to live in homes that give comfort and instill pride of ownership."

Rooted in Middle Eastern architecture, Swan's desert home has four vaults that tie into a main gallery space, forming an H. The carport has a palm-frond roof. A low adobe wall with a decorative cap screens the carport from the front of the house. The homeowner placed a sculpture by Arden Scott in front of the entrance to the main courtyard.

chapter 2

RAMMED EARTH

ASK OWNERS OF RAMMED EARTH HOMES WHY THEY like their particular type of house, and they will probably cite reasons ranging from energy efficiency and environmental benefits to the sheer romance of living within thick earthen walls. Since the late 1970s, an increasing number of people in the United States and other countries have been drawn to using rammed earth walls for their homes, whether simple, small owner-builder projects or elaborate multimillion-dollar estates designed by top architects.

Despite this recent resurgence of interest in rammed earth, the building technique dates back thousands of years. Essentially, it involves tamping down a moistened soil mixture under high pressure in a rigid boxlike form to create a rock-hard wall. It is one of the oldest forms of engineered walls known to mankind.

Around the world, earth was among the earliest building materials, particularly in areas where wood was in short supply. Babylonians, Sumerians, Assyrians, and other cultures built everything from basic shelters to elaborate monuments of rammed earth. Portions of the Great Wall of China, dating to 700 B.C., were originally fortification walls built of rammed earth. In 221 B.C.,

stone blocks were added to reinforce and unify the earthen wall, which snakes from Central Asia westward to the Yellow Sea. Pliny the Elder, the first-century Roman writer, historian, and naturalist, wrote of walls in Africa and Spain "stuffed" with earth.

Phoenician traders brought the rammed earth tradition to the Roman Empire, as far north as what is now England. Rammed earth walls could be built in virtually any climate, as opposed to adobe, or mud blocks, which required a certain number of dry, sunny days to form. Throughout Europe—particularly England, Germany, and France (where rammed earth is called *pisé de terre*)—examples of centuries-old rammed earth structures still stand.

European explorers and settlers took rammed earth to the New World. In St. Augustine, Florida, the oldest European settlement in the United States, the sixteenth-century Spanish explorers used a mixture of ground seashells and earth pounded into wooden forms to construct buildings. Portuguese and Spanish explorers took this form of rammed earth to South America, and English settlers brought rammed earth to Australia.

In the United States, particularly along the East Coast, rammed earth was a relatively popular building technique throughout the late 1700s and into the 1800s. It was often used by farmers and plantation owners, who had plenty of labor—and earth—to create homes, outbuildings, slave quarters, and other structures. The Church of the Holy Cross in South Carolina, built of rammed earth in 1850, still stands today.

By the end of the nineteenth century, the railroad and the availability of materials including lumber, brick, and glass put an end to the interest in building with rammed earth. Rammed earth resurfaced in the 1920s and particularly in the 1930s, during the Depression, when the U.S. government promoted the building technique as being inexpensive and offering a way to put available labor to work. Various rammed earth "subdivisions" were designed and built around the country. Even architect Frank Lloyd Wright, a proponent of bringing quality housing to the masses, designed a rammed earth housing community for the Detroit area in 1941, though it was never built due to the onset of World War II.

Between the material shortages of the war and the postwar housing needs of returning GIs, interest in rammed earth once again diminished as frame-construction subdivisions sprang up across the country.

During the 1970s, several cultural factors once again brought about an interest in rammed earth. People became concerned with ecology and the environment, and the Arab oil embargo forced the realization that energy sources were indeed finite. Additionally, in many parts of the world, the zeitgeist embraced a "back-to-the-land" movement, which encouraged people to follow nontraditional lifestyles, build their own homes, and become more self-sustaining.

The rammed earth resurgence was global. CRATerre, the Center for the Research and Application of Earth, was founded in France in 1979. The organization has subsequently offered a master's degree in earth architecture through the School of Architecture in Grenoble. Rammed earth also took off in Australia due to the scarcity and high cost of lumber and a quick acceptance of the technique by local building officials—and the public.

In the United States, builders, owner-builders, and architects began experimenting with rammed earth during the 1970s, particularly in the West. Several proponents of rammed earth have largely been responsible for bringing the technique into the mainstream consciousness. This group includes David Easton, a Stanford University engineering graduate, who built his first rammed earth project in 1975. Along with his wife, Cynthia Wright, Easton has written several books about rammed earth, given lectures and workshops, and developed new technologies to make rammed earth building more efficient. His more than one hundred and fifty buildings range from large private homes to factories, institutional buildings, and housing in Third World countries, where he also teaches local residents to do their own construction.

Easton's counterpart in southern Arizona is Quentin Branch of Tucson, whose interest in rammed earth sprang from a lifelong passion for organic gardening. With former partner Tom Schmidt, another rammed earth pioneer, Branch built his first project, a chapel for the Holy Trinity Monastery, in 1978. Branch, who has also spent years refining the earth-ramming process, has done in excess of two hundred projects, from bank buildings to luxury homes. A rammed earth retaining wall and sound barrier for a streetscape in Scottsdale, Arizona, is one of his largest public works projects to date.

In New Mexico, architect and adjunct professor of architecture Paul McHenry, Jr., established the nonprofit Earth Building Foundation in 1995, which is affiliated with the University of New Mexico's school of architecture. The foundation's mission is to collect and disseminate information globally on rammed earth and adobe building. McHenry received a National Endowment for the Arts grant to study the origins of earthen architecture and spent a year researching its history.

Other builders have become established throughout the West, particularly in California, Arizona, New Mexico, Colorado, and Texas. At present, about twenty builders in the United States specialize only in rammed earth, but as the method gains acceptance, that number is expected to grow.

From the standpoint of architectural style, the early rammed earth buildings were simple, straightforward, and, occasionally, bunkerlike. As techniques became more refined, creative professionals began to incorporate rammed earth walls into their designs, which, in recent years, have ranged from European-influenced architecture to ultracontemporary structures in which the walls are used almost as sculpture within a building.

Most builders follow the same general procedure to build a rammed earth wall. A concrete foundation is poured, as is a stem wall, which protrudes above grade some six to eight inches. The rammed earth wall adheres to this stem wall through gravity and pressure.

The builder must carefully select the right soil. Organic topsoil is not used to build walls. Instead, mineral-laden soil is used—a mixture of mostly sand with some clay. Tests are usually done to determine building viability. When the on-site soil doesn't work— as is often the case—soil must be imported from another locale, such as a quarry. The soil is mixed with a small percentage (usually 3 to 10 percent) of portland cement for stabilization, then is moistened with enough water to lubricate the soil particles and aid compaction. This stockpile must be kept evenly moist and mixed while awaiting use for the ramming process. The mixing can be accomplished by using anything from shovels and rototillers to machinery such as a skid loader.

Ramming forms are similar to those used for forming concrete panels. Basically, a form is boxlike, made of plywood and held together with metal straps. The depth of the form determines the depth of the walls, usually eighteen to thirty-six inches. For a two-story building, the first-story walls are often wider. The forms are set into place atop the stem walls. Electrical and plumbing lines are usually run within the forms; windows, doors, and other openings are framed out. In areas with seismic activity, building codes require the addition of steel rebar for the walls.

At this point, the moistened soil mixture is placed into the forms, usually with a tractor scoop or skid loader, then the soil is spread out. This is called a "lift," or a layer or course of soil. Lifts are usually done in eight-inch-high increments, and each lift is rammed. The ramming devices can be mechanical tampers—heavy weights at the end of a pole—but most American builders use pneumatic tampers, with tamping heads that vary in size for maneuverability. The eight-inch lift is rammed down to about five inches high, creating rock-hard density. If the forms are wide enough, workers can get down into the forms to do the ramming. This process is repeated up to the top of the wall form, at which point a bond beam, most commonly steel and concrete, is put into place to reinforce the strength of the rammed earth wall. Once the finished wall section has been rammed, the walls are stable, and the forms can be removed and reused to build other wall sections.

The finished walls have a slightly textured surface resulting from the kind of soil used and the striations left by the ramming process. Wall color also depends upon the soil mixture. Many homeowners find the natural texture, striations, and color desirable and simply use a clear sealant on interior walls to prevent dust and flaking. Others choose to plaster or stucco the walls. In high elevations or cold climates, builders often add a layer of rigid foam insulation to the exterior walls, then cover it with stucco. Because the top of rammed earth walls should be protected from moisture, many builders and architects choose pitched roofs with overhangs or cap the top of the rammed earth walls with tiles, bricks, or a layer of cement stucco.

Many builders have developed their own techniques and variations. David Easton innovated a form of ramming that involves shooting the soil mixture out of a high-pressure hose against a form, which reduces the time and labor costs associated with ramming. Other builders incorporate straw into the soil mixture. Yet another process, called cast earth, involves mixing the soil with a gypsum product to achieve a concretelike consistency. The mixture is pumped into forms to create a cast-in-place wall.

Building with rammed earth does come with a few caveats. The walls are more expensive to build than conventional frame walls, due to the labor-intensive process. With all other aspects being equal, a home with rammed earth walls may cost 5 to 15 percent more overall than conventional construction. Because of the rigid forms used, it's difficult, if not impossible, to create the rounded, sculpturally shaped walls that can be achieved with other materials. Extra insulation is needed in colder climates. Soil selection must be done carefully, and when soil is used from the building site, relandscaping must be considered. The walls are best built by experienced, licensed contractors; otherwise, it is possible to get cracked, out-of-plumb walls.

Nevertheless, there are many positive elements to rammed earth construction. Properly sited and designed, a rammed earth home is ideal for passive solar strategies. The thick, dense walls act as a thermal flywheel, gradually absorbing the warmth from the sun as the day wears on, then slowly releasing the heat into the interior at night. In a cold climate, a bank of south-facing windows and heat-absorbing flooring, such as tile or concrete, can add to the passive solar warming. In a hot climate, carefully shaded windows block the sun during the summer months, helping to keep the house cool. Many owners of rammed earth homes cite low monthly heating and cooling bills as big advantages.

Still other aficionados point to aesthetic reasons for using the material—the thickness of the walls, the natural-looking beauty of the surfaces, and the feeling of mass, sound absorption, and secure comfort that comes from the density of the walls.

WRIGHT-EASTON RESIDENCE

Napa, California

More than a century ago, European settlers were drawn to the inland valleys of California's north coast. They discovered that the Mediterranean climate, with its sun-drenched days from late spring through early fall and plentiful rains in the winter months, was perfect for growing grapes for wine. The valley floors were soon planted with acres of grapevines, and the settlers built homes, wineries, and other structures reminiscent of their European roots—large, thick-walled buildings, often with French, German, or Italian design elements. The wine country north of San Francisco was born.

It was here, in Napa, California, that David Easton and his wife, Cynthia Wright, chose to build a Provençal-style home in rammed earth. Sited at the edge of a creek, their two-acre lot is dotted with madrone and oak trees and surrounded by vineyards at the base of Mount George.

That they would chose rammed earth for their home is natural. Easton, an inventor, engineer, and builder, and Wright are partners in Rammed Earth Works, a company Easton founded in 1975 specializing in rammed earth construction. Since the early 1970s, Easton has been a proponent of rammed earth, authoring books on the topic, lecturing, and constructing more than one hundred

The residence's architectural elements, reflected in the dark-plastered pool, were inspired by old buildings from the south of France. Garden walls are constructed from "rebound," the soil mixture left over from making the home's walls, which is then formed into blocks.

and fifty rammed earth buildings. Easton met Wright in 1982 when he built her rammed earth home.

Though previous Rammed Earth Work residential projects had been interpretations and variations on the ranch house and Craftsman-Style bungalow, Wright and Easton chose to explore Mediterranean architecture for their Napa home, which they felt was appropriate given Napa's climate and European influences. They traveled to Europe and spent time in Provence, a region in southeastern France, where they researched the architecture, taking copious notes, photographs, and sketches of building elevations, plans, and details.

Collaborating with San Francisco architect Mike Baushke, Easton and Wright planned a 3,000-square-foot, two-story main house, a 1,200-square-foot guest house, studio, and garage and a small workshop, all set around a large courtyard that would serve as an exterior living space, complete with patios, pool, lawn, garden areas, and outdoor dining room.

For the main house, Easton and Wright created an informal, farmhouse-style plan. The front entry opens onto a short corridor. To one side is an intimate living room, anchored by a fireplace and opening onto the outdoors through French doors. To the other side is a combination dining room and study, complete with bookshelves and another fireplace. The master suite is just off the dining area, as is the country-style kitchen and pantry. A staircase in the corridor leads to second-story bedrooms, bath, and sitting area for the couple's six children. The guest house features a first-floor sitting room, bedroom, bath, and kitchen. A small, loftlike second-floor studio doubles as extra sleeping space.

To build the walls, the couple chose the new earth-ramming technology that Easton invented and has been using since 1990. Easton calls it PISE, an acronym for "pneumatically impacted stabilized earth," inspired by the French term for rammed earth, *pisé de terre*. Based on the gunite technology used to build swimming pools, PISE involves spraying the soil mixture against a form, as opposed to the traditional method of tamping the soil mixture into a form. Easton believes that the speed and efficiency of PISE can significantly reduce the cost of rammed earth construction.

Wright and Easton set up one-sided forms against which a worker with a high-pressure hose shot out the moistened soil-cement mixture in a twenty-four-inch-high

Opposite: Though the home is built by spraying the soil mixture into a form, more traditional cast earth was used for the window and door surrounds at the front entry.

Above, left: Throughout much of the main house, the walls were left un-plastered to show off natural coloring and texture.

Above, right: A small window, framed by a cast-earth surround, directs a shaft of light into the guest house.

Above: An east-facing courtyard off the kitchen is a sunny place to have breakfast. The basin of the trough-style fountain is made with "rebound," the soil mixture left over from making the home's walls.

Opposite: Vibrant colors enliven the farmhouse-style kitchen. The beams and light fixtures are from an old warehouse, and the wood for the island was recycled from old bowling alley lanes.

layer. Another worker followed closely behind, shaving and shaping the just-sprayed mixture to the desired thickness. The pressure is so strong that the soil particles are compacted against one another to create a rock-hard monolith. The process was repeated until the walls were full height. Electrical and plumbing lines were set in place prior to the application of the soil mixture, as were openings for windows and doors. In keeping with the area's seismic building codes, steel reinforcing bars were placed into the walls.

The smooth side of the walls—against the form—made up the interior walls of the main house, with the exterior walls remaining a rougher, stuccolike texture. The interior walls were sealed to prevent dust inside the house. For the guest house, studio, and garage, Easton and Wright reversed the forming, shooting the mixture from the inside out, resulting in a smooth exterior wall. The rough interior walls were covered with an integrally colored plaster, ultimately creating a smooth wall on the inside as well. The natural, mottled ginger color of both structures' exterior walls was the result of the soil, which was sourced from a nearby quarry.

Once the walls were done, Easton and Wright detailed the exteriors with clay tile roofs, sage green wooden shutters, and iron balcony railings, in keeping with the style of Provence. Metal arbors attached to both main and guest house provide support for grape and kiwi vines to grow and create shade.

Inside the main house, interior details were kept rustic and simple. Rough-hewn wooden beams define the ceiling. Cast earth was used to form the lintels; window, door, and fireplace surrounds; and crown moldings. The flooring throughout the house was also made by Easton and Wright. The one-and-a-half-inch-thick soil-cement tiles, which they call "terra tiles," are sealed and waxed for durability and to impart a subtle sheen. The home's eighteen-inch-thick walls allowed plenty of opportunities for niches and inset shelving for the display of art, books, and flowers. Though most of the main home's interior walls are natural rammed earth, the couple chose a warm, melon-colored plaster for the kitchen walls, further defining the space and reiterating the Provençal theme.

Because the architecture is strong and simple, little was needed in terms of furnishings and accessories. Easton and Wright were able to utilize many furnishings from

Left: A short entry hall connects the living room, dining area, and stairway leading to the upstairs bedrooms. The homeowners made the soil-cement tiles used throughout the house; radiant heat warms the floors.

Above: A narrow staircase leads from the entry hall to the upstairs bedrooms. Recesses and niches hold flowers and candles.

Above, right: Hooks set
into a wall recess serve as
a simple entry closet.

Left, above and bottom:
From the cast-iron tub in
the master suite, a bather
can view a distant mountain
and surrounding vineyards.

Above: The natural color of the home's walls have depth and appealing texture.

Top, right: Integrally colored plaster gives the kitchen walls a deep terra-cotta color. Niches provide shelf space for pottery and other artifacts.

Opposite: The dining room doubles as a library and study area for the school-age children.

their previous residence, including Mission-Style chairs and a farmhouse-style dining table and dining benches. Artwork includes folk pieces collected on their travels.

Throughout the house, the couple worked in many energy-saving strategies and recycled materials, as they do with all the homes they construct. There is no mechanical heating and cooling. Instead, the house has radiant-heat flooring, and cooling is accomplished via old-fashioned cross ventilation. Additionally, the rammed earth walls and soil-cement flooring absorb heat during the day, releasing it into the house during the cooler evening hours. Fluorescent lighting in portions of the house keeps energy usage low and doesn't add extra heat.

The beams are recycled from an old warehouse in Oakland, California, the kitchen cabinetry is made from old lumber, and the kitchen island uses the wood from old bowling alley lanes. The kitchen's warehouse-style light fixtures are just that—from an old warehouse.

The overall plan allows the family to move through the house on an east-west axis throughout the day, making as much use of the exterior spaces as interior. Weather permitting, an east-facing patio is a good spot for coffee and breakfast. By late afternoon, the west patio,

accessible through French doors in the living and dining rooms, is an inviting place to unwind and view the courtyard gardens.

Those gardens are an ever-evolving project for Wright in particular, who has been aided in their design by Thomas Nemcik, a Napa-based organic gardener and horticultural consultant. Together, they have been working on revegetating the woodsy perimeter of the property, amending the postconstruction soil, and attracting native wildlife and pollinators back onto the land, in addition to creating plantings and an orchard closer to the house.

Much of the inner courtyard's hardscape was also made using rammed earth, including the garden walls and the outdoor dining table and barbecue. Retaining walls separating the lawn and pool areas were built from "rebound," the small amount of soil mixture that bounces off a PISE wall as it is being built. The rebound is shoveled up and formed into blocks.

Between the two of them, this is the sixth rammed earth home Wright and Easton have built for themselves. They think there might be just one more at some time in the future. The major difference between this and the next one? Less square footage, more gardens.

BARRIO NEIGHBORHOOD

Tucson, Arizona

Above: A small portal provides a colorful spot where homeowners and neighbors can exchange the day's news.

Opposite: Flush to the street, the barrio homes combine architectural elements from historic downtown Tucson buildings and vivid colors from Mexico with modern earth-ramming technology.

Downtown Tucson has always been a tightly knit, culturally diverse neighborhood. The Spanish arrived in the area in the 1500s to find agrarian Pima Indians raising crops on the banks of the Santa Cruz River. By the late 1700s, the Spanish presence was made permanent with the construction of an adobe presidio established to protect settlers from attacks by aggressive Apaches. Mexico inherited Tucson from Spain after the revolution of 1821, and by the time it became part of the United States with the Gadsden Purchase of 1853, Anglo settlers had begun to drift into the area.

Many of the Anglos married into long-established Hispanic families, and residential neighborhoods, or *barrios*, began springing up at the edges of the commercial districts. The early barrio houses were built in an architectural style prevalent throughout southern Arizona and Sonora in northern Mexico. Flat-roofed and made of adobe blocks, the homes were flush with the street in front and opened onto an enclosed courtyard in back. The courtyards were often shared by several families as outdoor cooking and workspaces, fostering a close sense of community. Many of these homes were used as "town homes" by ranching families, who came in periodically

Opposite: A bright red door
and yellow exterior plaster
make a welcoming entrance
to the Wuelperns' home. The
thick, street-side rammed
earth walls muffle the sounds
of passing cars and pedestrians.

Below: Cow skulls found in
Mexico line up next to a
small pass-through window
connecting the family room
to the dining niche in the
Wuelperns' home.

from far-flung ranch lands to do business in Tucson.

With the arrival of the railroad in the late 1800s, these barrio homes became ornamented with milled lumber, glass, and bricks; wealthier families built more elaborate houses in other neighborhoods. Downtown Tucson's neighborhoods continued to thrive until after World War II, when returning GIs and those who had spent military training time in Arizona bought homes in the expanding suburbs.

After several decades of decline, the barrios came back to life as urban professionals began renovating the historic structures, discovering the ease of living close to the business district and the nearby University of Arizona campus.

Builder Tom Wuelpern chose to live here in 1990, joining a wave of urban pioneers coming back to the city's core to renovate and revitalize the old homes, many dating back to the late 1800s. Unlike most of his downtown neighbors, however, Wuelpern opted to use his skills as a planner and as a rammed earth and adobe builder to create a new neighborhood within an old district.

Wuelpern, who has degrees in architecture and environmental planning, first became interested in rammed earth and adobe building techniques in 1980.

Working with a rammed earth company, he learned to design, build the walls, and run the crew. By 1985, he had become a licensed general contractor and launched his own rammed earth and adobe building company with a partner in Tucson; in 1990, he formed his own company, Rammed Earth Development.

Although much of Wuelpern's business is the design and construction of new custom homes in Tucson's suburban areas, he had lived downtown and liked the ethnic mix of the barrio and the historic styles of architecture. During the course of living downtown, Wuelpern explored the Santa Rosa barrio, which has been occupied by Anglo, Chinese, and Hispanic families since the late 1800s. He discovered a series of lots—essentially one city block—that had never been built upon and decided to create his own neighborhood.

Wuelpern started with his own 1,300-square-foot rammed earth home and a spec home next door. During the next several years, friends and acquaintances began buying into his vision, and he built more single-family homes, as well as apartment and commercial buildings. To date, there are twelve new barrio buildings on the block, ranging in size from 1,300 to 2,400 square feet.

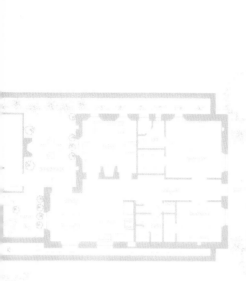

Left: An antique candelabra adds golden light to the bathroom. The claw-foot tub was found at a salvage yard.

Opposite: An eclectic array of furnishings creates a pleasant atmosphere in a master bedroom in one of the barrio homes.

Eleven are rammed earth and one is adobe. When the project is completed, there will be fifteen homes and buildings in the new neighborhood.

Along the street elevation, Wuelpern mixed the architectural motifs, but all buildings are based on what might have been built in the area between approximately 1880 to 1920. No two are alike. Some are flat-roofed, flush-to-the-street homes resembling early barrio residences; others have adapted Arizona's Territorial vernacular, with hip roofs and covered front porches. All have courtyards hidden from the street either to the side or at the back. Following Mexican tradition, Wuelpern colored the exteriors vividly with pumpkin, eggplant, purple, and tan stucco, trimmed with teal, red, or orange window and door surrounds.

Wuelpern's one-story home is typical of how he built the other homes. The street-facing walls are twenty-four inches thick, helping to muffle sounds of passing cars and pedestrians, while side and back walls are eighteen inches. Using traditional rammed earth forms, Wuelpern built the walls atop a concrete stem wall, using soils from a nearby commercial gravel yard. Because he was covering the walls with colored stucco on the exterior and plaster inside, the color and striations of the rammed earth wall were of little consequence.

From the street, the flat-roofed home—except for the discreet garage set to one side—looks as if it could have sprung up in the late 1800s. Two double-hung windows are set symmetrically on either side of the entry door. Aluminum *canales,* or drain spouts, spill water from the roof onto the gravel below; Wuelpern has dubbed these "parapet rockets" because of their form and the way they protrude from the roofline. An old-fashioned factory lamp illuminates the doorway, which, like the window surrounds, is painted bright red.

The front door opens onto a small living room, warmed by a fireplace. A guest bedroom and bath are also located in the front, or street side, of the house. A short hallway leads back to the kitchen and family room, behind which is the master suite. Two walled courtyards on either side of the house provide outdoor living space.

Wuelpern continued the historical theme with eleven-foot-high ceilings clad in unpeeled pine vigas and saguaro rib *latillas,* a ceiling treatment that dates back hundreds of years in the Southwest. Brick flooring throughout keeps with the rustic theme, as do the antique Mexican

Right: An assortment of found chairs gives character to the Wuelperns' small dining niche off the kitchen. The ceilings are made of unpeeled pine vigas. The deep-set, south-facing windows are part of a passive solar strategy, allowing sunlight to warm the brick floors during winter months.

doors installed in both bedrooms. More double-hung windows throughout the house add to the old-fashioned feeling. They were mounted flush with the exterior walls, allowing the thick walls to be appreciated indoors through deep window reveals.

Though Wuelpern concentrated on building in a historical context, his home, like the others he built in the neighborhood, came part and parcel with environmentally friendly aspects. The brick flooring and expanse of south-facing windows provide passive solar heating in winter; deciduous trees planted in the courtyard shade windows and walls in summer. Additional winter heat comes from fireplaces and a wall-mounted furnace. The water heater is solar. Tall ceilings and the long, narrow plan of the house create a cooling draft. There is no air-conditioning. Instead, Wuelpern relies on an energy-efficient evaporative cooler and ceiling fan.

Wuelpern scrounged salvage yards for recycled materials in keeping with the style of the house. He found an old claw-foot tub for the guest bathroom and planed down the floors of an old railroad boxcar to create butcher-block countertops for the kitchen. A vintage stove and refrigerator were finds from a used-appliance shop.

Once Wuelpern finished the house, he began furnishing it with Mexican art, antiques, and collectibles. In 1998, Wuelpern married, and his wife, Heather, a color consultant and expert in decorative paint finishes, began contributing her touches to the decor. Heather Wuelpern has added painted wall finishes, accessories, fabrics, and painted furnishings to the mix, infusing the setting with more vibrant colors and textures. Romantic candelabras now coexist harmoniously with a collection of horseshoes; lace coverlets have proven to be a pleasing counterpoint to old wood.

As much as the Wuelperns enjoy living in their rammed earth home, they appreciate living in a tightly knit community even more. They know everyone—their wedding reception was a block party, complete with a local band. Tom Wuelpern's office is around the corner, in the neighborhood's commercial building, so the commute is measured in footsteps, not miles. In addition to two-career couples and working professionals, the neighborhood has attracted families with young children.

The new construction has had an impact on the existing neighborhood, too. More older homes are being renovated, and a grocery store, which for years had its wares dwindle to cigarettes and liquor, is once again offering produce and other fresh foods.

Though Tom Wuelpern continues doing his custom rammed earth and adobe homes throughout Tucson and the state, the barrio project is obviously nearest and dearest. The social aspects of this project, he points out, have become just as strong a component as the architecture—which is why people live in neighborhoods in the first place.

Above: A native prickly pear cactus grows next to an adobe garden wall.

Opposite: Tarahumara pots, horseshoes, and a red chile ristra add Southwestern touches to the Wuelperns' living room.

McGEE RESIDENCE

Durango, Colorado

Above: Dry-stacked sandstone was used to form flower beds and walkways around the front and east sides of the house.

Opposite: Large slabs of sandstone fit together to form the front walkway. Snapdragons, cosmos, black-eyed Susans, and other colorful flowers are planted in the front bed. The homeowner uses the covered front porch as an outdoor room during the warm months.

Southwest of Durango, Colorado, heavily forested hills are interspersed with meadowland and rocky crags. Bald eagles call this home, as do black bear, elk, deer, and the abundant songbirds. At dusk, porcupines and skunks can be seen scurrying across the roads. The elevation here exceeds 7,200 feet, which means snowfall is heavy and stays on the ground longer than at lower elevations. This was once an area with cattle ranches, almost all of which have been sold off or developed into smaller parcels of land. Lynn McGee bought three acres in this rural locale and initiated her plans to build a healthy home, a place she hoped would feel as natural to her as when she goes camping.

The idea was not a new one for McGee, an avid fan of environmentally oriented architecture. She had designed and helped build healthy living spaces before, in Boulder, Colorado, with different materials but to the same end. Her goal has always been to use products that do not emit toxic gases (known as off-gassing) or waste natural resources, and to create an energy-efficient design that has an intimate relationship with the natural surroundings.

The style and type of construction McGee finally settled on took its cues from a workshop she attended in Santa Fe, New Mexico, given by Robert Laporte. Laporte teaches classes on building "Eco-Nests," with a technique that combines some elements of straw bale construction with traditional earth-ramming methods.

Adapting a plan from Laporte's Natural House Building Center, McGee chose a two-story design reminiscent of a gable-front house from the early 1900s. Entry is on the northeast side where it catches the morning sun. The active part of the house—the kitchen, living, and dining space—is on the first floor. The kitchen is small and efficient with windows on both northeast and southeast sides for daylighting. The dining area, which opens up to the second floor, is in the center of the first floor. At the southwest end of the house is a cozy living area. The bathroom/laundry is also downstairs, off the entry. Two small bedrooms are upstairs.

Invisible from the main road, McGee's Durango house is set behind a low hill at the end of a narrow dirt drive that skirts a forest of ponderosa pine and oak brush. Parking is a short walk from the main entrance, preserving the natural areas around the perimeter of the house. With the siting and pitched roof, earth-colored

walls, forest setting and front flower garden, the house has some resemblance to a Bavarian cottage.

Through Robert Laporte, McGee arranged to have the construction of the house serve as one of his workshops, providing participants a chance to learn traditional timber framing and the technique of light straw-clay. In exchange, thirty participants gave McGee a hand in building her home.

Construction began with an exposed timber frame structure, using lumber McGee found regionally. In lieu of nails, traditional wood joinery was used to assemble the posts and beams. Nontoxic linseed oil and citrus oils were applied to seal the raw wood. The final coat of oil was mixed with beeswax.

Wheat straw bales, found in the San Luis Valley in Colorado, were used to create the walls, along with the addition of a slurry of local clay, sand, and water, blended in a concrete mixer. The baling wire on the straw bales was snipped, the bales were broken apart, and the slurry was added. The straw was then tossed with a pitchfork, like a salad, until it was evenly coated with the clay mixture. Pitchforks also came in handy for loading the straw-clay mixture into plywood forms attached

Opposite: A large, open space downstairs has ample daylighting from numerous door and window openings.

Above, right: Both bedrooms upstairs open up to a walkway and the center of the house. Muslin curtains can be drawn for privacy.

Right: The timber frame structure is visible from the inside of the house. The well-functioning, compact kitchen includes a refrigerator that costs less than forty dollars a year to run.

to the timber framing. McGee then packed and tamped the mixture by using her feet and then two-by-twos or two-by-fours, being careful to compress the corners. The walls set up fast enough to remove the plywood forms immediately from the lower level and reset them for the next, higher level. Horizontal bamboo rods were inserted through predrilled holes in the posts and embedded into the straw-clay mixture for added strength. After the walls were finished, the plywood forms were washed for reuse in the roof construction.

The ratio of clay to straw varied, depending on the location of the walls. The south wall, which the winter sun would hit, needed more thermal mass and therefore a higher percentage of clay. The north wall would receive no direct sunlight, so more straw was added for insulation.

For the interior walls, McGee chose a nontoxic plaster made from kaolin clay, fine silica sand, cooked wheat paste, and natural mineral pigments. She needed to wait more than three months to plaster the outside, allowing time for the walls to dry throroughly. For the exterior plaster, McGee followed a recipe concocted by Laporte. The ingredients—a combination of clay, sand, cooked wheat paste from high-gluten organic flour, and finely chopped straw—were mixed to the consistency of butter. McGee also added fresh cow dung to the exterior plaster, believing it creates an enzyme action that is helpful in making a breathable plaster, which allows trapped moisture to evaporate.

Part of the interior first-level flooring is sandstone. The mud floor chosen for the dining and living area gives the house a direct connection with the earth. For the mud floor, McGee started with an eight-inch base of pumice rock that was tamped and compacted, then a layer of straw-clay was added. A rough coat of mud was followed by several finish layers before the floor was sealed with linseed and citrus oils. The final coat of oil contained blood meal. The pine flooring in the upstairs bedrooms, was also sealed with linseed and citrus oils.

The finished structure is open, airy, and efficient, filled with natural light from skylights and numerous windows. A wide countertop with a stove and a food preparation area divides the kitchen from the dining area. A southeast window wall turns the dining area into a greenhouse space and opens to the outdoors via a French door. McGee wanted the living area to be more intimate and

A small garden shed to the east of the house holds tools, bags of soil, and other garden supplies.

gave it lower ceilings and used less glass. A compact wooden stairway leads to the upper floor, where a walkway with open railings overlooks the dining area. White muslin draperies, rather than solid doors, can be pulled across bedroom openings when privacy is needed.

Furnishings are a simple mix of antiques, overstuffed chairs, and a sofa. Plants line up against the dining room window wall. A few eclectic rugs and some well-chosen art pieces finish off the interior.

For the working mechanics of her home, McGee chose propane as the energy source for her radiant floor heat, an energy-efficient refrigerator that costs approximately thirty-four dollars a year to run, and an on-demand hot-water heater. She also purchased a Swedish washer and dryer known for water and energy efficiency.

Outdoors, a raised flower bed, outlined with dry-stacked sandstone, is planted with native flowers that bloom during the summer months. The patio and covered porch are paved with sandstone set in sand. When weather allows, this is the center of activity, where McGee and her visitors can hear and see the wildlife, and smell pine resin and moist earth—a combination she finds intoxicating.

Not long after McGee moved into her straw-clay house, she began planning her next project, thinking of ways to be even more effective in her campaign to build healthy living spaces. Her contagious enthusiasm has infected other residents in the area who are willing to join her in a new venture using green architecture. This time she will try a co-housing development with open areas where residents share responsibilities.

INDOOR/OUTDOOR RESIDENCE

Tucson, Arizona

Above: The home is set in the open desert west of Tucson. Views include the city and distant mountains.

Opposite: The home's mass was broken into three separate buildings, each offset from one another. Open-air corridors link the three buildings.

Not far from downtown Tucson, the Tucson Mountains rise up to form a western frame for the city and a final resting spot for desert sunsets. Dense stands of tall saguaros, native cacti, dot the hills and mountains, as do palo verde, mesquite, and creosote bush. Coyotes, bobcats, and javelinas, along with the more elusive mountain lion, call the area home.

For several decades, the private landowners on this west side of town have tended to be mavericks and desert enthusiasts, who have snapped up large parcels of pristine desert land to keep the landscape intact. Drive up and down the winding, dipping gravel roads, and you won't see many large homes or subdivisions. Houses built here have tended to be more experimental and environmentally sensitive. One neighbor may live in a straw bale house; another may have active and passive solar systems in an adobe house.

This mountainous Tucson neighborhood was a natural site to build Arizona's first exposed—that is, unplastered—rammed earth home. Not only did the residence utilize the earthen material in a new way, but its living quarters were also set up in an interesting configuration. Three separate buildings contain the "rooms"; outdoor

breezeways function as hallways.

The unusual characteristics of the house stem from a collaboration between the homeowner, who is an attorney, and the architect, Paul Weiner, both of Tucson.

In 1989, after years spent living in an older home near Tucson's urban center, the homeowner bought some four acres of pristine desert in the Tucson Mountains. For five years, he spent evenings and weekends on the land, camping out and hiking in the nearby mountain park, contemplating the nature of the property. Eventually, he began building subtle pathways through the acreage and placed benches for rest and views. A devotee of yoga and meditation, he also erected a sweat lodge on the site and invited friends and colleagues to share his desert preserve. Eventually, it became clear that any house he built would have to fill three needs—fit into the desert, provide a private retreat, and offer spaces to share with friends and the community.

The owner asked Paul Weiner to shape his needs into a tangible form. Weiner, who has practiced architecture and building in Tucson since 1979, is well versed in alternative building materials and approaches. He has built numerous straw bale homes, worked with solar energy,

Opposite: Thick, rammed earth walls, sandblasted concrete, and heavy wood beams form a strong composition in the corner of the meditation room.

Right: Prickly pear and saguaro cactus flank the dark-plastered, solar-heated lap pool. The pool and the adjacent bathroom pavilion are the latest additions to the home.

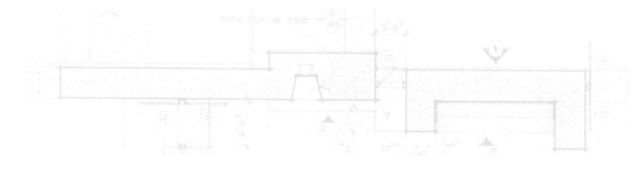

and incorporated recycled materials into many projects. When the homeowner indicated a desire to incorporate the proposed house into its desert setting, and also mentioned an interest in achieving a quiet, monastic ambience, Weiner began to think about rammed earth.

He was familiar with the works of Quentin Branch and Tom Wuelpern, two innovators working in Tucson with rammed earth, but up until that point, all the walls they had built had been covered in plaster or stucco. Weiner became fascinated with the natural striations and aged look of the uncovered earthen walls. Both the owner and Weiner agreed to build the home of rammed earth—and to leave the walls exposed.

A building site was easily identified just above the arroyo that cuts through the land. The view axis would be east toward the city below and west toward the mountains. Two wildlife paths meandered right through the spot where the house would stand. Weiner proposed breaking up the home into three separate buildings, thereby keeping the wildlife corridors open by situating them in the breezeways between the buildings.

The home's form became three simple boxes, set side by side, yet offset from one another. Weiner placed the

Opposite, far left: The rammed earth walls were set onto a sandblasted concrete stem wall.

Opposite, left: Thick rammed earth walls serve as stairs to the roof, which has views of the surrounding mountains and city below.

Right: A ramada made of steel beams and matchstick bamboo shading creates one of several outdoor "rooms." The low garden walls are made with rhyolite, a locally quarried volcanic rock.

most public of the three buildings at the north, closest to the main approach to the house. The owner uses the 400-square-foot space for meditation and yoga, or for the workshops and meetings he likes to host. The 650-square-foot middle building was designed to contain a kitchen and a small living room. The southernmost structure—700 square feet and the most private—holds a master suite and a home office. The plan, Weiner notes, gently coerces the owner outdoors many times as he goes through the normal routines of the day. Additionally, each building has patio areas that expand the living areas.

The design motif for the three buildings came about as a collaboration between Weiner and three architectural associates, Rick Joy, Lauren Clark, and Suz Weisman, who worked with him at the time. Inspired by the sculptural strength of the rammed earth walls, they kept the home's elevations simple and decided to let the material speak for itself.

Quentin Branch came on board to do the walls, which he built onto a sand-blasted concrete stem wall, using traditional wood-ramming forms. Some six hundred tons of soil for the walls came from the site, excavated to make a building pad, and about three hundred tons came from

another local source. The golden-hued walls are eighteen inches thick and range in height from about twelve to twenty-one feet. As the ramming forms came off, the owner rubbed the exterior surfaces and corners with a brick to erase the vertical and horizontal lines left by the forms and to enhance the striations of the walls. The technique helped the new walls look aged, a desired effect. Once the rubbing was completed, a clear acrylic sealant was used on both interior and exterior to prevent flaking and dust.

The roof was designed to be flat and parapeted. The rammed earth parapets were sealed with a cement-based plaster to prevent water seepage. The roof, angled slightly to encourage water runoff, is sprayed-on foam covered with a gravel ballast that not only protects the foam from ultraviolet rays, but also makes the roof walkable for future use as a sundeck. Channels in the roof drain rainwater into decorative scuppers set into the rammed earth walls and, in turn, into concrete troughs, which serve fountains at the entrance to the breezeways and along the patios. Heavy chains dangling from the roofline also lead rainwater toward the ground.

The mass of the walls is punctured by French doors

and windows of various sizes, set at differing heights to let in light and capture views. Scored concrete serves as the simple floor material, and sandblasted, oiled structural steel is used for lintels, for the hood over the range, and as an element to bring in ductwork and lighting to the island dividing the kitchen from the living area. Western red cedar and pine beams add interest to the ceiling in all three buildings; in the meditation room, the ceiling is built in the form of a recessed pyramid. Rustic cabinetry throughout the house is made of rough-sawn fir, outfitted with custom hardware. Patio areas are enclosed with low walls made of rhyolite, a locally quarried volcanic rock.

Energy-efficient evaporative coolers and heat pumps in all three buildings can be turned off and on as the spaces are in use. In the middle of the summer, when humidity levels are up and evaporative coolers are no longer efficient, the owner uses an air-conditioning system in the bedroom to make nights more comfortable. Radiant floor heat warms the interiors, as does a pellet stove in the meditation room and traditional fireplaces in the other two buildings. Water is heated by six solar panels, and a backup gas heater kicks in on cloudy winter days.

Against the simple strength of the architecture, furnishings are minimal. The meditation room is empty, except for a specially made area rug. A few comfortable chairs and a sofa furnish the living room, and the kitchen is enhanced by the addition of striking leather and steel bar stools designed by Tucson furniture designer Max Gottschalk. The master suite is spare, divided between sleeping space and office by a freestanding closet and cabinet system.

Though the home had a building envelope outside of which the natural landscape remained unscarred by construction, the land closer to the house needed to be revegetated after the house was completed. The homeowner did the work himself, rescuing desert natives that were in the paths of neighbors' construction projects and replanting hundreds of them around his lot, including bursage, creosote, jojoba, and cactus varieties. The idea was to make the house look as though it had grown up in its setting.

After the home was finished, the owner married and made a few additions. As it had only one bathroom, located in the master suite, Weiner designed a guest bath. Rather than being incorporated into the rest of the

Opposite, far left: Ocotillo branches, lashed together with metal bands, create a natural enclosure for the outdoor shower outside the master bath. The branches will eventually take root, leaf out, and bloom.

Opposite, left: Rough-sawn cabinetry has enough character to stand next to the texture of the earthen walls. The range hood is made from sandblasted, oiled structural steel.

Left: A counter divides the kitchen from the cozy living space. The sandblasted, oiled structural steel element above the counter houses ductwork for the evaporative cooler as well as light fixtures.

house, it is a freestanding indoor/outdoor pavilion, built of rammed earth, wood, and rusted corrugated metal. Though the toilet and sink are under the roof, the shower stall, clad in galvanized metal, is without overhead protection, giving bathers views of mountains and the home's rammed earth walls. The guest bath doubles as a ramada for the dark-plastered lap pool, also a recent addition. As both husband and wife occasionally work from home, there are future plans for a guest bedroom and home office structure, also of rammed earth.

Though the house was originally designed for one occupant, its physical presence gives pleasure to both husband and wife. They enjoy the feeling of solitude and silence that the home's walls afford, yet like to share their home with friends, family, and community. They spend as much time outdoors as in, using patio spaces as living and dining rooms, hiking in the desert, or swimming laps in the pool. Most of all, they say, they like that their house is, in essence, simply another form of the desert.

LOW RESIDENCE

Scottsdale, Arizona

A rammed earth wall extends from the house to provide a backdrop for the dark-plastered, negative-edge pool.

In north Scottsdale, the Sonoran Desert becomes lush as it rises into the foothills of the McDowell Mountains. Palo verde and mesquite trees, creosote bushes, and saguaros and other cacti dot the rolling landscape and line the dry washes. After winter rains, spring wildflowers add splashes of indigo, yellow, and crimson to the landscape's pale hues. In ancient times, Hohokam Indians settled portions of the land; petroglyphs, pueblo ruins, and other remnants of their agrarian civilization can still be found in the area. More recently, ranchers ran cattle and sheep across what was then sparsely populated expanses.

It was here, overlooking the expanse of metro Phoenix to the south and west, that Linda and Mickey Low chose to build a winter home, a retreat from their primary, East Coast residence. They purchased a ten-acre parcel in the mid-1990s and began plotting a home spacious enough for the two of them, their three large dogs, and regular visits from their grown children, other family members, and friends.

Besides space, the only other item on the agenda was that the home be contemporary. The home turned out to be the first permitted rammed earth house built in Scottsdale, and it subsequently won numerous design awards. The design elevated rammed earth to a new level, where the walls are used as much for their sculptural properties as for their practical and environmental benefits.

The design and materials stemmed from the Lows' choice of architect. Edward Jones of Phoenix is known for his innovative, contemporary designs and for his choices of experimental materials. With his partner, brother Neal Jones, Eddie Jones is also known for utilizing salvaged, recycled, and industrial materials, as well as seeking out environmentally friendly products for building. The practice won numerous awards and recognition for its 1994 design of an environmental showcase home for Arizona Public Service, the local utility company. The Phoenix house, which is open to the public, was built entirely with recycled and energy-saving materials.

By the time Eddie Jones met with the Lows, environmental issues in building were second nature to his designs. He spent time on their land, determining which course would be best to give them the large home they desired, yet also planning how to blend it into the fragile desert landscape.

Rammed earth seemed appropriate for the project. Jones had studied the material when he was a student in the 1970s at Oklahoma State University, and he knew of its rise in popularity, especially among a handful of builders in Tucson. Jones and the Lows took a road trip to Tucson to meet with builder Quentin Branch and view several rammed earth projects. As they headed out of town, they pulled into the first restaurant they spotted for a quick dinner. Its name was Dirtbags and the specialty was "dirt burgers." It seemed, as Jones recalls, cosmically ordained that the Lows' house be built of rammed earth.

The house turned out to be about 7,500 square feet. Even with using rammed earth walls to blend the house into the site, Jones's challenge was to make sure the house didn't sit in one massive block on the land. Instead, the architect broke up the various functions among several buildings, creating a compound that was easier to nestle into the desert.

The main house is organized along an east-west axis, with living and dining spaces, family room, kitchen, and study in the center of the plan. Guest bedrooms and baths were placed to the east. To keep the master suite private from the rest of the main house, Jones created a separate pavilion to the west, on the opposite side of an arroyo that bisects the property. The master suite pavilion is linked to

Opposite, clockwise from top left:

Maple and cherry cabinetry marks the sleekly efficient kitchen. A narrow ridge skylight runs the length of the house and dapples a silver-leafed bulkhead with shafts of sunlight. The ceiling is clad in fir; flooring is polished concrete.

The subtle hues of prickly pear cactus are highlighted by the golden color of a rammed earth wall.

A sandblasted block fireplace with a cantilevered concrete hearth provides a sculptural focal point in a corner of the living room.

The four walls of the study just off the dining room are rammed earth. Artwork is suspended by wires from the ceiling to avoid hammering into the earthen walls.

A spiky ocotillo reaches for the sky next to the rusted metal and rammed earth walls of the garage.

A sandblasted glass coffee table and Mies van der Rohe's Barcelona chairs are the simple furnishings in the living room, which overlooks the pool patio. The glass panels atop the rammed earth walls separate the living room from the guest bedrooms.

the main house by a long hallway that functions as a bridge across the arroyo. A small, freestanding guest house is just across a private courtyard, off the north side of the house. The four-car garage, also a separate building, has its back to the home's main approach, its rear wall becoming a backdrop for plants and trees, making it nearly invisible in the landscape. Across from the garage, a simple, two-vehicle carport provides extra shaded parking and a place to wash cars.

Quentin Branch came in from Tucson to build the walls. Although a portion of the soil for the walls was taken from the property, the majority—four hundred tons—came from a nearby flood-control project. As granite boulders were being removed to build a water-retention basin, heavy equipment ground them up into decomposed granite, a rough mix often used in landscaping to mimic the desert floor. Branch mixed the moistened granite-based soil with portland cement and used traditional wooden ramming forms to build the eighteen-inch-thick walls, which range in height from nine to seventeen feet.

The walls were set onto a sandblasted block stem wall, a variation of the more common concrete stem wall. In

another twist on traditional rammed earth construction, Jones opted not to have electrical and plumbing set into the walls. Instead, where plumbing and electrical met rammed earth, the lines were set outside the walls and covered by maple panels, floated out from the walls. In the bedrooms, these maple panels also serve as headboards.

The wall color has a gold hue and sheen due to the mica content of the granite. As the walls were to be left in a natural form without stucco or plaster, Branch used a clear acrylic masonry sealant on the exterior and interior to prevent dust and sand particles from coming off the walls.

In elevation, the house is influenced by the long, low ranch houses historically associated with Arizona, particularly the form of the pitched, corrugated metal roof. In some spots, long expanses of earthen walls bisect window walls, which flood the interior with natural light and provide views of desert, mountain, and city. Some exterior walls are clad in rusted metal, another element that seems at home in the arid climate. The only spot in the house where rammed earth forms all four walls is in the central study, which Jones created to be a sheltering nook for the couple.

Cast-aluminum barstools reflect the late afternoon light in the bar area of the family room.

Inside, Jones juxtaposed the rustic walls with sleeker materials, including a smooth, polished concrete floor, maple and cherry cabinetry, granite countertops, and a fir-clad ceiling. A bulkhead along the ceiling line that houses the ductwork was silver-leafed by local artist Randy McCabe.

Other notable design elements mark the house. An eight-inch-wide skylight runs the length of the house at the apex of the roof, casting an ever-changing shaft of light throughout the day. A cantilevered fireplace in the living room has a glass cutout that allows the flames to be seen in the study. Small windows in the study and along the wall of the master suite's bridge are paned in colored glass, which creates geometric rainbows as the sun's rays pass through. A tranquil pool cools a hidden courtyard next to the overscale front entry door, which pivots open. Stretches of sandblasted glass provide translucency and privacy.

Even with the emphasis on design, energy efficiency and sustainability were factored into the home. As the Lows occupy the home primarily during the winter months, the thermal characteristics of the rammed earth walls are ideal for their needs. The walls absorb heat during the day, then release it into the interior at night. Banks of south-facing windows and the concrete flooring combine to provide passive solar heat; during the summer, natural light is controlled with corrugated metal overhangs. Insulated, filtered glass shields the interiors from heat and ultraviolet rays. The galvanized metal roof made from 60 percent recycled material, is lightweight, heat-reflective, and durable. Doors and windows are positioned for cross ventilation. Overall, the home is easy to maintain.

The furnishings are simple and spare. Jones designed a sandblasted glass dining table and coffee table for the living room; other pieces include modern classics, such as Mies van der Rohe's Barcelona chairs. Several contemporary paintings are ingeniously hung against the rammed earth walls from wires suspended from the ceiling.

Most of the native desert vegetation on the site, which includes tall saguaro cacti, was undisturbed by the home's construction.

The landscape was kept natural, and areas scarred from construction were revegetated with native plants. A small lawn was added off the guest bedroom wing, ready for future grandchildren. Each room in the house has access to a courtyard or patio, each with its own viewpoint and ambience. The largest patio, accessible from the living and family rooms, serves as an outdoor dining spot for barbecues and is near the black-surfaced, negative-edge pool, whose surface reflects the house and sky.

Though the Lows have now spent several winter seasons in their rammed earth home, they still revel in its views, its sense of tranquility and security, and its free-flowing space. Each day, Mickey Low says, they find something new they had never noticed before—a design detail, a shaft of light, the way the shadows cast patterns on the earthen walls. The most ringing endorsement of rammed earth comes from the architect. He subsequently built his own home of the earthen material.

chapter 3

STRAW BALE

THE ORIGINS OF STRAW BALE CONSTRUCTION MAY HAVE been quite simple. Farmers in cold climates stacked bales of straw to line the walls of wood or rock barns. The straw was a good insulator and it kept the livestock warm through the winter months.

Today, homeowners, builders, and architects have put their own spin on farmers' early instincts. Since the early 1990s, straw bale has become an increasingly popular building material for homes and commercial structures. With the increasing number of straw bale buildings going up, particularly in the western United States, references to the "Three Little Pigs" are on the wane, and more municipalities are including the construction technique in their codes. Devotees cite everything from environmental attributes to the emotional response of being in a straw bale structure as reasons for building with this material.

Put simply, straw should not be confused with hay, which is herbage, such as alfalfa or other vegetation grown for animal feed. Straw is what's left over after rice, rye, barley, wheat, and other grains are harvested. It's indigestible and tough. Other than using it as bedding for animals, most farmers consider it a waste product.

Although loose straw, mixed with clay or other materials, has served as a building material for centuries, the use of bales didn't come about until the late 1800s, after the invention of the baler. This farm machine cuts and compresses the straw, then ties it with wire or twine into large blocks, usually forty to fifty inches long, twenty-three inches wide, and sixteen inches high.

At the turn of the century, pioneer farmers on the prairies of Nebraska and South Dakota began taking advantage of the baling machine not only to help with the harvest, but to create blocks of straw to build walls for homes and outbuildings. As trees and lumber were scarce in the area, the bales provided a quick and easy way to erect a shelter to protect a family from the prairie's summer heat and howling winter winds. The bales were stacked to form walls; the roof was often poles covered with sod. Once the occupants realized how comfortable the buildings were, the bales were covered with plaster and made more permanent.

Though interest in straw bale building continued well into the late 1940s—spreading into Wyoming and even Alabama—the technique carried with it a bumpkinish whiff and even connotations of poverty. Once the occupants began moving up the economic ladder, straw bale homes were quickly abandoned in favor of modern, more "sophisticated" building materials such as masonry or frame and stucco. Nonetheless, as a testimonial to straw bale's soundness, many of the homes and buildings built as early as the 1910s still stand today, particularly in northwestern Nebraska where the technique first began.

As with many other rudimentary building materials, including adobe blocks and rammed earth, straw bale construction waned after World War II, as subdivisions sprang up across the country to accommodate returning GIs and the subsequent baby boom. It wasn't until the 1970s when the first glimmers of straw bale's renaissance emerged, stemming mainly from the back-to-the-land, self-sufficiency ethos that had begun coloring a segment of American culture. Even then, it was just a glimmer. There was a small cottage built in the late 1970s in Washington, then another in northern California. A few articles were published in local and regional magazines, inspiring a handful of other builders to use straw.

In 1981, Athena Swentzell Steen built a straw bale home outside Santa Fe. The experience led her to write books and sponsor workshops on the topic, along with her husband,

Bill Steen, and colleagues David Bainbridge, an ecologist, and builder David Eisenberg. By the late 1980s, newsletters, workshops, and media coverage began to spread straw bale's newfound popularity. Straw bale structures began going up in Arizona, New Mexico, California, Colorado, Texas, and other states. The interest spread to Canada, France, Finland, Mexico, and Central America. A workshop even introduced straw bale building to rural Russia.

Nonetheless, straw bale was still viewed with some skepticism by many local American building officials, who viewed it as experimental. Many of the buildings from the late 1970s to the early 1990s were "bootleg," built without permits or approval from authorities, usually in rural areas. Proponents of straw bale's virtues, including architects, engineers, environmentalists, and builders, worked diligently to prove the material's worth via field tests and research. By 1991, straw bale buildings began receiving official building permits—and they had been proven worthy of bank financing and insurance. As of the early 1990s, there were probably only several hundred straw bale buildings, mostly in the Southwest. Now that the building technique has been legitimized, that number is expected to balloon exponentially.

Straw bale homes are evolving stylistically as well. While the homes built in the 1980s and early 1990s were mostly owner-builder scenarios, recent projects have been the experiments of design professionals. The early homes were often simple, one-story square or rectangular plans with pitched roofs. Except for the basic styles of the early straw bale homes of the prairies, the material did not come with an architectural pedigree, as did adobe. Today, anything goes for this wall material. Straw bale designs are contemporary, organic, or even designed to fit into a historical context. Constructing multiple stories and mixing straw bale with other wall structures isn't unusual, either.

Basically, two types of straw bale walls can be built. One is called "Nebraska style," or load-bearing, built the way the early homes on the prairie were constructed. With this method, the weight of the roof and any aboveground floors is supported entirely by walls of stacked bales. The bales are placed atop one another in a running bond—with each bale set atop the vertical joint of the two bales beneath it—and then are pinned. The roof plate is connected to the foundation via straps, cables, wires, or rods.

The type of straw bale wall most accepted by local building officials is the non-load-bearing wall, more commonly called "post-and-beam" construction or "straw bale infill." For this method, a structure made of wood, masonry, concrete, steel, or other material supports the weight of the roof. The bales simply form the wall between the posts. Builders have the choice of stacking the bales flat or on edge, which results in a slimmer wall, desirable for some architectural styles. For load-bearing walls, bales must be stacked flat for stability.

For either type of wall, the construction sequence starts with a foundation as wide as the bales of straw and elevated above grade to protect the bales from ground moisture. Additionally, the top of the foundation should be moisture proofed, so any wetness from the ground is not absorbed by the bales. Rebar pins are spaced around the foundation to impale and set in place the first course of bales. As other courses of bales go up, they're pinned together strategically with more rebar, wood, or bamboo pins. In areas prone to earthquakes, the walls can be further braced with threaded rods and metal straps placed diagonally on both sides of the stacked bales.

For load-bearing walls, door frames are attached to the foundation, and window frames are installed as the walls go up (bales can be cut or stacked to accommodate the sizes). For non-load-bearing walls, door and window frames are often built into the supporting structure. Windowsills in both wall types must be moisture proofed, as should the tops of the walls. For both walls, electrical and plumbing lines can be laid between the bales as the walls go up, tucked in later, or even set into the bales in channels made with a chain saw or other sharp tool. Many builders try to place plumbing lines outside the straw bale walls to prevent problems from possible leaks.

Straw bale walls do settle, and builders have found that an eight-foot wall can lose several inches in height—possibly more if it's a load-bearing wall, once the roof is in place. Some builders opt to speed up the process by mechanically precompressing the walls. In any case, once the walls are up, any leftover cavities can be stuffed with loose straw, and corners and openings can be trimmed before the walls are usually wrapped in wire mesh for application of stucco or plaster. Some homeowners choose siding or drywall to clad the bales. In a few cases, pioneering homeowners decide to leave the interior walls uncovered.

Other variations of wall systems include mortaring the bales together and retrofitting an existing building with interior or exterior straw bale walls.

Straw bale construction has many positive attributes and a few caveats. It is environmentally friendly in that the walls recycle an agricultural waste product. Straw is still burned in many areas as a method of disposal, and utilizing it as a building material theoretically cuts down on air pollution. A plastered, two-foot-thick straw bale wall has an insulative value of R-40 to R-60, proponents say, significantly higher than the average American home. However, the efficiency of a home's insulation also depends on the nature of the windows, doors, and roof.

Building a straw bale wall is relatively easy and relatively inexpensive as far as wall systems go, and therefore has attracted a significant number of owner-builders who put up the walls over the course of a weekend, like an old-fashioned barn raising, with the help of friends and family. For many, building their own straw bale home is an empowering and life-changing experience. A two-thousand-square-foot home uses approximately three hundred bales of straw at a cost of four dollars to six dollars per bale. Despite the success of several straw bale homes built for stupendously low costs (completely with owner labor), most straw bale homes will cost as much as the average custom home, factoring in a professional builder and whatever creature comforts, finishes, and details are deemed necessary for the project.

Potential problems from fire, pests, and moisture always come up in discussions of straw bale construction. Though loose straw is highly flammable, and care must be taken during the course of construction, a finished plastered wall is quite fire-resistant. Tests have proven that the bales are so dense that they lack the oxygen necessary to induce combustion. Experts use the analogy of trying to burn a telephone book. Proponents also point out that insects and rodents are less interested in living in a straw bale wall than a typical frame wall. Once the walls are properly sealed, there's no digestible matter for them to feed.

Moisture is a trickier issue. Bales should be free from excessive moisture (there is a tool that can be used to test the moisture level) and should be stored dry until needed. This means that the bales must be elevated from the ground and protected from rain until the walls are finished and, of course, that proper construction tech-

niques must be used to prevent moisture from entering the walls. Except for the foundation, tops of walls, and windowsills, which should be covered with a moisture barrier, straw bale walls need a breathable plaster or other wall covering to allow moisture to escape from the bales, rather than trap it inside. If the bales are too moist once the structure is built, the straw can deteriorate, which is a big problem for load-bearing walls and can leave any stucco or plaster unsupported. Molds can also be released, causing respiratory irritations for some residents. Good building techniques, though, prevent these problems.

Owners of straw bale homes and buildings usually have lists of reasons why they love the material. Recycling, energy-efficiency, sound absorption, romance of the thick walls, and pride in building something different from the norm are often on the list.

In many cases, a casual visitor may never know that the home or other building is made of straw. That's where the tradition of the "truth window" comes into play. A small area of the interior wall, left uncovered with sheetrock or plaster, is framed in and covered with glass or a little door. One peek reveals what's inside the walls.

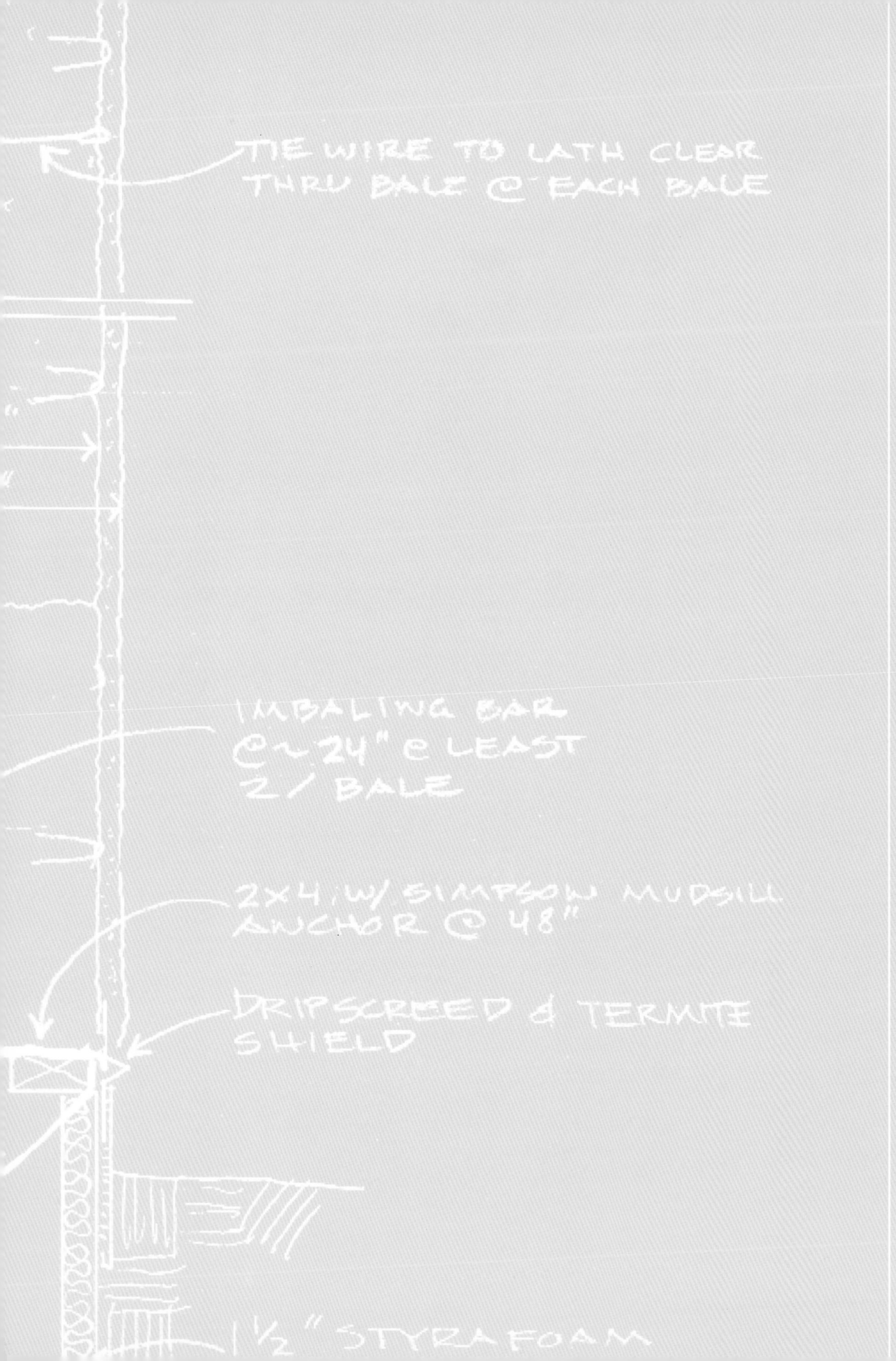

TIE WIRE TO LATH CLEAR
THRU BALE @ EACH BALE

IMBALING BAR
@~ 24" @ LEAST
2 / BALE

2X4 W/ SIMPSON MUDSILL
ANCHOR @ 48"

DRIPSCREED & TERMITE
SHIELD

1½" STYRAFOAM

HARDING RESIDENCE

Tucson, Arizona

Right: The bungalow style of the straw bale house was designed to blend with the turn-of-the-century neighborhood. The wildflower garden blooms from early spring well into summer.

Above: Set in the back, the garage mimics the form of the house, but is clad in galvanized, corrugated metal, typical of old sheds in the neighborhood. During peak spring bloom, the backyard wildflowers almost overwhelm the garden path and patio.

In 1880, the Southern Pacific Railroad came to Tucson, linking the desert town to the rest of the United States. The railroad brought with it jobs, opportunity, "civilization," and prosperity. The town grew, and as its residents climbed steadily toward middle and upper class, new neighborhoods developed north and east of the old barrios, or downtown residential districts.

Armory Park near downtown Tucson was one such neighborhood that sprang up as a direct result of the railroad. Many of its early residents were Southern Pacific executives and engineers; the railroad had shops and other facilities built within a short carriage ride of the enclave. Reflecting the new wealth and the civilizing factor that the transportation link provided, the early denizens built homes that emulated architectural styles found in larger, more established cities. Between approximately 1880 and 1920, when Armory Park flourished, homes were built with Queen Anne, Mission Revival, bungalow, and Spanish Colonial Revival motifs. The railroad also made a wide range of building materials more readily available. Armory Park homes were among the first in Tucson to utilize fired bricks, milled lumber and trim, and window glass in their construction.

Although all residential neighborhoods near downtown Tucson waned in popularity after World War II, Armory Park, like the other urban neighborhoods, experienced a renaissance beginning in the late 1970s. Today, the neighborhood's residents represent a multicultural, multigenerational mix, and many of the homes are being restored.

Julie Harding liked the history, the mix, and the convenience to downtown that Armory Park represented. Most who walk by her bungalow-style home with its inviting front porch and sunny wildflower garden think that it is an excellent restoration project, another old house lovingly rebuilt. Harding's house is new, however, and it was built with straw bales, a material never used before in this historic neighborhood.

Harding, who works in the airline industry, got hooked on Tucson's downtown and on straw bale construction when she rented a small house in a nearby historic neighborhood. The house was built of straw bales, and Harding liked the thick walls and the sense of quiet and serenity the structure imparted. She also enjoyed being able to walk to nearby restaurants, shops, and cultural events. After finding a narrow, L-shaped lot in Armory Park, Harding asked the architect and builder of the

house she had rented to help her build her new home.

Architect Paul Weiner of Tucson was already quite experienced with straw bale—he had designed close to fifty such structures, mostly in southern Arizona, ranging from quite conventional to experimental. Builder John Woodin, also of Tucson, had been building straw bale homes since 1994, in addition to doing rammed earth and adobe construction.

For Harding, Weiner designed a modified shotgun floor plan. The public spaces—kitchen, dining area, and living room—of the 1,660-square-foot home face the street. A corridor leads back into the rear garden. On one side of the corridor is the master bedroom, to the other a guest bedroom and bath. A front porch extends the living space.

Architecturally, the house is what Weiner calls "Sonoran bungalow," with thick walls reminiscent of the region's historic desert architecture. The bungalow style is evident in the raised foundation, front porch, hip roof, traditional wood trim, and casement windows. The idea was to blend the new house, in both scale and style, with what already existed up and down the street. Most of the houses near Harding's were built in the 1910s through the 1920s and were small to medium in size.

Opposite, far left: The builder made the vivid tiles used in the bathroom. A stainless-steel countertop is a modern contrast to the rustic pottery and folk art from Mexico.

Opposite, left: In the dining area, pigskin table and chairs reiterate the home's Latin American theme. The painting is by Tucson artist Frank Franklin. The tablecloth and lace curtains are Guatemalan.

Left: The builder made the cobalt blue tiles for the living room fireplace. The pigskin chair was a local find; the sabino wood armoire is from Nogales. Ceiling fans throughout the house help keep utility bills low.

Though Harding was interested in all aspects of her home's construction, she left the actual work in the hands of Woodin and his five-member construction crew. Woodin started the process with high concrete stem walls to create a raised foundation. Harding's walls were raised eighteen inches, rather than using stem walls extended some six inches above grade as for many straw bale homes. Although there had been some discussion about creating a crawl space beneath the house, Woodin felt that the weight of the walls was too heavy not to have full support, so the void was backfilled with dirt.

A post-and-beam framework was created, and some 250 bales of wheat straw from a Tucson feed store were used to build the walls between the frames. Woodin was careful to keep moisture out of the bales during construction and used a moisture meter to make sure the bales were dry enough to use. The first course of bales was impaled on rebar protruding from the stem walls, then subsequent courses were strategically pinned together with more rebar pins. Woodin tied the bales to the posts with baling twine to add rigidity to the walls. The walls were covered with a wire mesh for plaster. The exterior walls were covered in a warm, gold-hued cement

Top, left: A wrought iron
bed and armoire from
Mexico add a festive note
to the master bedroom.
The fabrics are Guatemalan
textiles.

Bottom, left: Yellow,
pumpkin, and teal add depth
to the kitchen's bead-board
cabinetry. The lamp was a
find in Nogales; the boxes
are from Guatemala.

stucco, the interior walls were finished in a creamy gypsum plaster.

The electrical was run in conduit along the base of the walls or, in some spots, placed in a shallow channel between the bale surface and the plaster coating. Plumbing lines were put in framed interior walls, except those for the kitchen sink, which run through an exterior bale wall. The pitched, asphalt-shingled roof has shallow eaves, which keeps rain off the walls.

Harding's home has conventional heating and cooling, but her utility bills are much less than her neighbors', owing to what Woodin estimates is the R-55 insulative value of the two-foot-thick plastered straw bale walls and the R-40 insulation of the roof. Dual-pane, low-emissivity windows add to the home's insulative value. In winter, the living room fireplace provides a lot of heat. During warmer months, Harding can open the front and back doors at opposite ends of the shotgun corridor to create a pleasant draft. Ceiling fans also help keep the interior cool until the dead of summer, when standard air-conditioning is a necessity.

The home is relatively small and simple, but it packs a lot of visual interest. Woodin set the windows almost

flush to the exterior, allowing deep window reveals on the interior. The reveals are splayed, so more light can bounce into the interior, and the edges are rounded for a soft, handcrafted effect. Harding, who travels to Guatemala and other Central American countries, enjoys deep, intense colors and made liberal use of Woodin's handmade, glazed ceramic tiles in deep green, blue, yellow, and red to accent the fireplace and clad the walls and countertops in both bathrooms.

Working with the cream-colored plaster walls and the neutral tones of the pine flooring, Harding added more color to the interiors with warm yellow cabinetry, trimmed in turquoise and pumpkin in the kitchen, a deep sage green bookcase in the living room, and window and door surrounds painted red, yellow, and blue.

Harding, who used to have a folk arts store in Tucson, filled the home with furnishings—both new and antiques—purchased in Mexico and collected over the years. For the kitchen, she created an island out of an antique cabinet from India and set a gas range into it. The Mission-Style sofa in the living room was made by local craftsmen. Harding covered the cushions and throw pillows with Guatemalan textiles.

The homeowner carried her love of colors outdoors. Working between an huge, old stand of prickly pear cactus on one side of the lot and a tall hedge of oleanders, Harding planted banks of flowers—including poppies, lupines, hollyhocks, and verbena—that bloom profusely from early spring throughout summer. The flowers envelope the front yard and flank the back garden's curving pathway leading from the house to the corrugated metal garage, which echoes the architecture of the house.

Harding has enjoyed settling into the house and watching the sun's rays shift across the deep window reveals. She likes the sense of quiet and peace that the straw bale walls afford, and also enjoys living in an urban neighborhood. Whenever she can, she relaxes on the porch, keeping up with the neighbors, who do the same.

Above, left: Near the entry, a Mexican table holds a collection of wooden santos, or saints, from Ecuador, Bolivia, and Guatemala. The armoire is also from Mexico.

Above, right: A vibrant Mexican tree-of-life candelabra lights up a niche in the hallway.

GANNETT RESIDENCE

Crested Butte, Colorado

In 1990, while Alison Gannett was studying and teaching at Solar Energy International, an institute in Carbondale, Colorado, that emphasizes alternative energy, she saw an issue of *Out On Bale*, a quarterly periodical that focuses on straw bale construction. Gannett was drawn to the idea of using straw, a renewable waste product with a high insulative value, and planned to build her own straw bale home someday. She wound up being the first person to build a Victorian-Style straw bale home in the National Historic District of Crested Butte, Colorado.

Originally raised in Peterboro, New Hampshire, Gannett pursued environmental studies at the University of Vermont. In 1989, after vacationing in Crested Butte, she fell in love with the skiing, the town, and the landscape. At Crested Butte, Gannett also learned how to build houses while working for an environmentally oriented design and construction company. Her job was to look at construction problems and figure out how to fix them. She is now a straw bale consultant, as well as a professional extreme skier.

Crested Butte is a place where cold winter air rolls down the slopes of the majestic snow-covered peaks and settles into the valley where the town is located. The town elevation is close to nine thousand feet, and the average January temperature is minus four degrees Fahrenheit. On some winter days, the temperature dips to minus forty or fifty. Summers are normally pleasant and mild. National forests and wilderness areas, including the Gunnison National Forest and Snowmass Wilderness Area, surround the town with thick stands of aspen, Douglas fir, and lodgepole pine. Because of its spectacular display of summer wildflowers, Crested Butte is known as Colorado's wildflower capital.

Like most mountain towns in Colorado, Crested Butte was founded as a mining center in 1879. Silver mines originally covered the nearby slopes, and stately Victorian homes lined the town's streets. By the 1880s, the silver had played out, but shortly thereafter, rich veins of coal were unearthed. More claims were staked, with one mine eventually employing more than four hundred men. Coal continued to be the economic base until 1952, when the last big coal mine closed and the future of Crested Butte was questionable. It wasn't until the 1970s that skiing came into vogue, not only providing an income for historic Crested Butte but supporting the newly constructed town and resort on

Above: The straw bale walls insulate against temperatures that average −4° F in January.

Right: In an area with fifteen-foot snowbanks, the homeowner chose a pitched metal roof to help shed the heavy snow load. The exterior is designed to blend in with the Victorian homes in Crested Butte's Historic District.

Opposite, clockwise from top left:

A kitchen counter separates the dining area and the kitchen. Pine was used for the flooring.

At the apex of the roof, the house is twenty-eight feet high. The straw bales are stacked around the outside of the post-and-beam structure, leaving the timbers exposed on the inside. The assortment of furnishings reflect the region's history.

The entry doubles as a greenhouse and passive solar collector. During winter, it captures direct sunlight that heats the scored and colored concrete floors and straw bale walls. The heat then rises up to the second-floor living, kitchen, and dining area.

A deep window ledge, created by the depth of the massive straw bale wall, offers seating in the master bedroom. In the winter, the first-floor windows can be completely covered with snow, which is the reason that the living area is located on the second floor. Furnishings were kept simple against the home's strong architecture.

Mt. Crested Butte, a 12,162-foot-high peak with long ski runs, condominiums, and shops for tourists.

Worried about its treasury of historic buildings, Crested Butte designated part of the town as a National Historic District in 1974. The architectural review board that oversees the district follows stringent guidelines detailing what can and can't occur within district boundaries. Gannett worked with these officials for two years before finally obtaining approval to build her home within those boundaries.

Set back from the street, Gannett's house is carefully placed between two Victorian homes on a small lot that has views of snow-dusted peaks to the north. Pine and fir trees cover many of the slopes to the west. Because the lot is flat, the house could be built without much disturbance to the building site.

Gannett designed a 1,288-square-foot, two-story home. From the street, entry is through a greenhouse space that opens onto a master bedroom, a guest bedroom, and a bathroom. To better capture distant views, Gannett chose to place living, dining, and kitchen areas on the second floor and a loft space above the kitchen. Views were not the only factor in this decision.

In winter, there can be fifteen-foot snowbanks against a house, leaving first-floor rooms virtually windowless—which Gannett decided would work better for bedrooms than active living areas.

From the outside, it's impossible to tell whether Gannett's house is new or old or that straw bales are underneath the earthen plaster. Nestled between the two existing Victorians, Gannett's house borrowed from their lines, using white wood trim and four-pane wood sash windows to connect the new home with the town's historic buildings. A steep pitched metal roof not only sheds snow easily, but mimics the rooflines of the district's other homes. Gannett's roof measures twenty-eight feet high with the loft, about the same height as neighboring houses, well within the district's height restrictions.

Construction began on June 15, 1997, and finished by October 31 of the same year. Serving as her own contractor, Gannett taught her subcontractors how to work with straw bales. Rather than using a traditional timber frame support system with dowels and pegs, which can be costly, Gannett went with locally milled four-by-four posts and beams for structural support and

Above: The homeowner, a professional extreme skier, stores her skis and jackets on a rack in the entry greenhouse.

The kitchen was designed in a U-shape with wood cabinetry built by a local woodworker. Solid maple countertops and a decorative tile backsplash highlight the kitchen. A high, north-facing window frames a view of Mt. Crested Butte.

set them inside the straw bales, leaving the bales stacked around the exterior of the posts. Gannett refers to her innovation as an "exterior straw bale wrap," an idea that saves time and labor, and stops air and moisture leakage. The wrap also eliminates the need to lath any joints and allows the exterior plaster to be applied directly to the bales. Wire is used to tie the bales to the posts with a trucker's hitch, or cinch-style knot.

Gannett's goal in constructing her home was to eliminate any unnecessary steps and expenditures. Another money saver was using a monolithic foundation accomplished from a single pour of concrete. At the same time Gannett poured her foundation and concrete floors, she also scored and colored the concrete to create a finished floor surface.

When the exterior walls were ready to plaster, earth and masonry sand was mixed with boiled flour paste and handfuls of chopped straw. The sand kept the mixture from cracking. The flour and clay in the soil acted as a binder and provided strength. The first coat of three layers that Gannett applied had more earth so it could stick to the bales. The following coat had more sand to reduce cracking, and the final coat, even more sand. For

the inside plaster, Gannett applied two coats of the exterior mixture, which is a dark earth color. For the final layer, she mixed a five-gallon bucket of drywall finishing compound and applied only one thin coat to lighten the walls to a natural buff color, a cost-effective, nontoxic way to pigment the walls.

Wrapping the straw bales around the outside of the posts left the posts exposed on the inside, providing an easy way for Gannett to attach interior walls, cabinets, and mirrors. Maple countertops highlight the hand-crafted natural wood cabinetry made by a local crafts-person. A wide kitchen counter serves as a divider between kitchen and eating area. Because Gannett is athletic, she chose to access the loft by way of wooden handholds on a post beside the kitchen counter, a rather primitive-style ladder. Two high windows over the kitchen sink frame spectacular views of Mt. Crested Butte.

In winter, blasts of sun penetrate the south-facing window wall in the entry-greenhouse space, heating the concrete floors. Hot air rises up the stairwell to the kitchen and dining and living areas, as well as the loft, where the warmth is absorbed. Double-hung windows use heat mirror glass with a low-emissivity coat of film trapped between the panes, adding insulation to an area that generally has high thermal leakage. The roof and a few interior frame walls—for the pantry and interior bathroom—use nontoxic straw and cotton insulation. Because Crested Butte can have days of extreme cold, Gannett also opted to have a backup system of hydronic radiant heat that runs through plastic tubing below the flooring. There is also a woodstove. A short growing season convinced her to grow vegetables and herbs in the entry greenhouse, giving the plants a year-round growing season, and raising the level of humidity in the cold, dry climate. Plants thrive in the entry greenhouse, a space that Gannet finds warm and comfortable.

All paints, stains, and glues used in Gannett's house were nontoxic, and products with formaldehyde were avoided. She chose energy-efficient, compact fluorescent lighting and energy-efficient appliances. The sinks were free for the taking, scrounged from nearby remodels.

An eclectic mix of furnishings from different periods decorates the house. The downstairs master bedroom has an old claw-foot tub, reminiscent of mining days, placed under a window that frames the spectacular landscape of mountains and valleys. Overstuffed chairs and a love seat occupy the living area. An antique table and chairs furnish the dining room.

Gannett landscaped her yard by scattering local wildflower seeds. She also planted native aspen trees and a small patch of grass in the front.

Most of the people who pass by Gannett's house have no idea that it is a passive solar, straw bale residence. Stately and elegant, it blends in with the other beautiful Victorian homes in the National Historic District of Crested Butte. Inside, Gannett stays warm and cozy, without the great expense for heating of most new homes at a nine-thousand-foot elevation.

WARKENTIN RESIDENCE

Marin County, California

Opposite: Seen from low on the hillside, the home rises out of the meadow grass. The exterior stucco was stained with iron sulfate to create a warm color. Chains hanging from the gutters lead rainwater down and away from the walls.

Above, right: Tucked into a meadow on a hillside, the home has sweeping views of the valley below. The design is influenced by old winery buildings in the area.

David Warkentin's fondest memories of growing up in Northern California include playing inside old winery buildings, where thick walls and the way light splayed in through deep-set window reveals imparted a sense of permanence and connection to the past. By the time Warkentin was ready to build his own home on a ten-acre site in Marin County, California, he knew its architecture would be influenced by those old buildings.

Warkentin, who works in the field of homeopathic medicine, also wanted to address environmental concerns in the creation of his home. His property, north of San Francisco, is on a hillside, with sweeping views of the valley below. In summer, morning fog often shrouds the undulating terrain; in winter, rains soak the land. During periods of drought, brushfires are not uncommon. Warkentin's land includes a grassy meadow, ringed by oaks, redwoods, and firs; his immediate neighbors are raccoons, skunks, foxes, opossums, and bobcats. No built object could ever match the natural grace of the hillside, Warkentin reasoned. Therefore, he decided to build small, and to build with as many recycled and environmentally friendly materials and systems as possible. He chose to build a straw bale home.

Warkentin contacted architect Sim Van der Ryn, who had taught at the University of California at Berkeley when Warkentin studied there. Van der Ryn, known as a proponent of ecologically sound architecture, assisted on the initial concept for the house, then suggested that Warkentin work with an associate, architect David Arkin.

With the homeowner's input, Arkin, who subsequently launched his own practice, chose a site in the meadow, which has views north and east. Complying with Warkentin's request for simplicity, Arkin designed an 1,150-square-foot plan that incorporates an open central living, dining, and kitchen space, a bathroom, and a bedroom/home office. The old wineries and local farm sheds gave rise to the home's simple architectural style, which Arkin detailed with a pitched metal roof, Craftsman-Style clerestory windows, French doors, and casement windows. The plan was to use as many recycled materials as possible for both structural components and finish details. Rice bales were chosen as the wall material.

The plan, however, took awhile to implement. Although straw bale structures had been permitted in other parts of California, at the time none had been given official blessing by Marin County building officials. According to

Above, left: Lanes from an old bowling alley provided wood for the dining nook table. The architect continued the theme with a housewarming gift to the client—a bowling ball made into a candle holder.

Above, right: Redwood cabinetry and a green concrete countertop add a rustic look to the bathroom. The homeowner did all the tile work himself. The shower is outdoors, just beyond the window, accessible by an exterior door.

Opposite: An open floor plan makes the small house seem more voluminous. Near the entry, a gnarled madrone trunk is used as a sculptural post. The dining nook is behind the half wall.

Warkentin, it took some nine months to obtain proper permits. Most of the delays came from concerns that the land was in a fire zone, and there were questions about the fire-resistant qualities of straw bale construction.

After months of looking into the research and testing done around the country on straw bale, Warkentin's home plans were approved in 1996, making his the first permitted straw bale home to be built in Marin County. Because Marin County officials eventually concurred that straw bale structures have proven to be extremely fire resistant, they went one step beyond issuing a building permit. The local fire marshal designated Warkentin's home a fire-safe haven for firefighters who might have to battle a brushfire in the area.

Once permits were issued, construction began quickly. Though a general contractor came in on the project, Warkentin chose to be very involved in building the house. Arkin designed the house to be post and beam, with the bales of straw used in-fill style. A concrete foundation was poured, lifting the walls above grade; a channel of pea gravel drains water away from the walls. The posts are vertical wood I beams upon which rest recycled redwood trusses. Once the post-and-beam frame

was set, Warkentin and a group of friends set the straw bale walls in the course of one day.

Rice straw bales, a by-product of local rice farming and plentiful in the region, have a high silica content and are a bit tougher on hands and tools than other types of straw. Because rice straw decomposes slowly, California farmers traditionally burned it as a waste product. The Environmental Protection Agency, however, has mandated a phaseout of the burning practice, leaving farmers with a lot of straw on their hands. The straw bale construction industry has become an environmentally sound recycling opportunity.

For Warkentin's home, the bales were laid on edge, stacked between the I beam posts, creating a slimmer wall than for other straw bale homes. The bales were pinned together with rebar for structural strength, then covered with wire mesh. Windows and doors were framed in and sealed for moisture, and electrical wiring was tucked between the bales—far back enough to prevent nails from being driven into the wiring. As a matter of prudence, Arkin designed the plumbing to go into a wood-framed wall in the bathroom and into a cavity below the kitchen sink. That way, any potential leaks would not harm the

Opposite: A tall window and a deep reveal in the living area provide an inviting spot for reading or napping. The homeowner's collection of Indian textiles and statuary add color to the space. The ceiling is clad in pressed ryegrass panels; the flooring is scored soil-cement.

Right: A hot tub, built into a cantilevered redwood deck, offers serenity and spectacular vistas.

straw bales. The only shower is outdoors, keeping moisture accumulation outside the house. The pitched metal roof sheds rain away from straw walls. Once all was in place, exterior walls were coated with stucco and stained with iron sulfate to create a pleasing warm hue. Interior walls were coated with a hand-troweled soil-cement finish.

Many other recycled or environmentally friendly materials were used in the home. The exterior wood cladding detail near the entrance and under the eaves is redwood recycled from old bridge timbers and wine tank staves. The ceiling is clad in pressed ryegrass panels, and the flooring is scored soil-cement, topped with red clay treated with linseed oil and carnauba wax. A gnarled madrone trunk, which had died of fire-blight damage, was used as a support beam in the kitchen area. Arkin found old doors for the home and incorporated wood from old bowling alley lanes into the kitchen counter and dining table.

Dual-glazed, low-emissivity windows add to the energy efficiency. Arkin estimates that the coated walls have an insulative value of R-50. Radiant floor heating, warmed by thermal solar panels, provides heat in winter months. Propane serves as backup heat for the water during periods of prolonged cloudiness.

The home is not only environmentally responsive but aesthetically pleasing. Large windows look out over the valley. The window reveals are deep enough to accommodate futons for overnight guests. Niches, open redwood cabinetry, and stretches of wall space allow Warkentin to display the textiles, crafts, and statuary he has collected during his many trips to India. The floor's natural hues frame his oriental rugs. Several "truth windows" in the walls neatly frame and reveal the straw walls. Access to outdoor spaces visually stretches the living space.

Since moving in, Warkentin has enjoyed his hillside refuge and the solitude it provides. He still has projects to finish. A six-hundred-square-foot bedroom was added, as were a meditation courtyard, a deck, a hot tub, and a pond.

The landscape has been nudged back to life where it was trampled by construction. Closer to the house Warkentin is growing a natural curtain of vines to provide privacy around the outdoor shower. He has broadcast wildflower and native grass seeds over the meadow surrounding the house and has had some unexpected help in landscaping as a result of building the house. Leftover seeds from the rice bales have sprouted on the hillside, creating his own private field of rice. The recycling continues.

BENNETT RESIDENCE

Jemez Mountains, New Mexico

The house looks out over a
vast meadow filled with
late-summer wildflowers.

Sky, forest, and meadow are part of the vista from the home's grassy courtyard.

Noel Bennett's straw bale home high in northern New Mexico's Jemez Mountains is snugged into the bowl of a hillside facing a meadow filled with grasses and wild-flowers. A small stream bisects the thirty-acre property, which is ringed by ponderosa pines, spruce trees, aspens, and oaks. Bear, elk, and coyotes amble across her land, which is adjacent to the Santa Fe National Forest. The region was once home to ancestral Puebloans; the ancient remains of their pueblos still dot the land. Bennett's land, at eight thousand feet in elevation, is often blanketed with deep snow during the winter. In the summer, late-afternoon thunderstorms refresh the air.

Bennett, author, artist, weaver, and nationally recognized expert on Navajo textiles, built the home with her late husband, Jim Wakeman. For the couple, building the home wasn't just a necessity to provide a shelter for living and working. It was a manifestation of their philosophy and of years spent researching the best ways in which to build lightly upon the land.

Wakeman, an engineer, and Bennett began their research in the mid-1980s, while they were building a small weekend retreat in a canyon not far from the present site. They enlisted the help of Minnesota architect Michael McGuire, who knew Bennett through collecting Navajo rugs. McGuire helped them design a structure that they could build alone, with minimum damage to the environment, and which would allow them to fully experience the surroundings.

While researching and building the retreat, Bennett, Wakeman, and McGuire found that little information was available about ecological building in wild places. In 1990, they conceived a project to study the concept and received a National Endowment for the Arts grant. Bennett and Wakeman crisscrossed the country, viewing architectural projects built with minimum impact on the land and interviewing architects and builders who kept environmental issues at the fore of their design philosophy. Their study, *A Place In The Wild,* distilled the philosophy of building on fragile sites into four main features—that the structure should have minimal visual, physical, and environmental impact and should open its inhabitants to nature, rather than seal them off.

When Bennett and Wakeman completed the NEA study, the logical next step was to build their own home following their established criteria. The land they found was the perfect place to test their philosophy. A small

The homeowner's komondor
welcomes guests at the
front door. The exterior
stucco was textured with
bits of straw, echoing the
wall material, then colored
with iron oxide.

vacation cabin from the 1930s had burned, leaving only charred log walls and a native stone fireplace. Two other small buildings—a bunkhouse and a barn—stood on the property, but other than that, the land was virtually untouched. Access was via a narrow dirt road. They could build upon the footprint of the old cabin without disturbing much new land, and the old road needed no further widening or embellishments. The bunkhouse provided them with a "camping" structure so they could spend time on the land observing its ecosystem before making final decisions about the house.

It wasn't long before they realized that architect Michael McGuire would be the best choice for creating the sustainable, energy-efficient, minimum-impact home they desired. Of all the architects they had met during their research, McGuire was most well versed in building in wild places. During the course of his career, he had built state park buildings, an environmental research center, and buildings for a wilderness camp, and had experimented with passive and active solar systems and new materials since the early 1960s. McGuire began traveling frequently to northern New Mexico to work on the house.

McGuire agreed that the best place to site the new

A fireplace from the old cabin that once occupied the site anchors the gallery. The floor is concrete and part of the home's passive solar strategy. Artwork is by the homeowner.

A black AGA stove warms the kitchen. Open shelving provides display space for colorful glassware and dishes.

house was where the old cabin had been—where hill and meadow met. The new house could curve around, opening southward onto the meadow for maximum views and solar gain, while turning its back against the cooler north side and, coincidentally, the roadway.

He designed a U-shaped plan, placing the master bedroom at the western end of the U, and an open kitchen and living area on the east side. A long gallery connecting both sides of the house was designed to display Bennett's minimalist paintings and the multimedia sculpture that she created in collaboration with Wakeman. The cabin's old fireplace serves as the anchor point for the gallery and for the house as a whole. A garage, a main workshop, and a lower-level workshop were placed behind the gallery, bermed into the bowl of the hill. Above the garage, there's a loftlike home office and a guest bedroom.

Though doing the plan was relatively easy given the homeowners' needs and activities, achieving their desire for a house that was part of the outdoors and at the same time sheltering was challenge for McGuire. He responded by opening up the gallery and the two wings of the house to the south-facing grassy courtyard and meadow beyond with large expanses of window walls and sliding glass doors, and keeping the window openings relatively small around the rest of the outside perimeter of the house. He dropped the eaves of the steeply pitched roof close to the ground at the back of the house and along the living room and kitchen wing, creating a greater sense of shelter—what Bennett has dubbed "the protective wings of a mother hen." In style, the architecture was mainly influenced by site, but also by the sensibilities of indigenous architecture and Japanese farmhouses that the homeowners and McGuire admired.

Choosing the materials was given much thought. At that high elevation, with temperatures sometimes dipping to minus twenty degrees Fahrenheit, good insulation was first and foremost. Straw bale walls were not only environmentally friendly, but proven to be superinsulative. Dual-pane windows and a well-insulated roof were also specified for the job.

When Bennett and Wakeman had decided to use straw bale, it was not yet accepted by state building officials. They later obtained one of the first experimental straw bale permits issued by New Mexico. With Wakeman serving as general contractor, construction on the house began in 1992, using mostly local labor. A building

A freestanding wall in the master bedroom serves as a headboard and separates the sleeping space from the closet and dressing area. Indonesian textiles cover the bed.

envelope was established, outside of which the land could not be disturbed by construction. Materials were brought in on the narrow road. This sometimes necessitated disassembling deliveries brought by large trucks and carrying supplies to the site by hand or with a small truck.

A concrete foundation and slab with radiant floor heat were poured, and the post-and-beam framework for the walls was built using formaldehyde-free, recycled wood products. Wakeman and Bennett tucked the straw bales, which they bought from a source in Colorado, in between the posts, then secured them together with stakes. The bales were covered with a wire mesh, which was "sewn" into the bales with baling twine threaded onto a long metal "needle" of Wakeman's design. The walls were covered with cement stucco, mixed with cut bits of straw for texture, and colored with iron oxide on the exterior to produce a deep neutral color that helps blend the home into the landscape. Interior walls were colored identically to achieve continuity between outdoors and indoors.

The pitched corrugated metal roof shades the walls and protects them from snow and rain. The roofline also provides visual continuity from exterior to interior. Heavy-gauge steel was chosen for the roofing. A lighter-gauge corrugated metal was used as the ceiling cladding throughout the interior. Twelve-inch-thick rigid insulation was layered between roof and ceiling.

McGuire's plan for the house follows hemicycle designs favored by Frank Lloyd Wright, an early proponent of solar architectural strategies and one of McGuire's major influences. Particularly in the winter, the sun warms the concrete floors of the master bedroom first, then moves through the gallery until it reaches the living quarters toward the end of the day.

The home's overall insulation is estimated to be about R-60, keeping energy costs low, even in the depth of winter. The radiant floor heat is cycled on by computer when needed. An energy-efficient stove stays on to warm the kitchen like an old-fashioned hearth. The old fireplace, however, was sealed and left as a reminder of what Bennett calls an archaic, low-efficiency heating method. In summer, the generous roof overhangs shade the sun from walls and windows.

The water supply system consists of a well with a low-energy, high-efficiency submersible pump that supplies a thousand-gallon cistern. Water is distributed to the house with a highly efficient jet pump. When the electricity goes

Exposed trusses and beams add to the strength of the interior architecture. The ceiling is clad in a lightweight corrugated metal, creating a luminous surface. The custom table pulls out of the kitchen counter to provide extra seating.

out (a relatively regular occurrence in this remote area), a back-up generator can power the whole house for several days. All the toilets are low-flush, and most interior lighting is electronically ballasted, compact fluorescent fixtures.

The home is a pleasing place in which to live. McGuire's design approach was more high-touch than high-tech. Trusses and beams were kept exposed indoors, adding to the home's architectural drama. Straw bale pillars were spaced at intervals to bisect the window walls around the grassy courtyard, reiterating the depth of the walls and evoking a mood reminiscent of a medieval cloister. The thick walls also provided opportunities to create deeply inset windows and niches for art.

Given the strong lines of the home's architecture and its natural setting, the interior furnishings were kept minimal. Built-in benches in the living room provide comfortable seating and views of kitchen proceedings and activities in the meadow. The kitchen counters double as a breakfast bar. A table of McGuire's design pulls out from within the counter for dinner. In the bedroom, a freestanding wall separates the bed from the closet/dressing area. Throughout the house, paintings, sculpture, a few antiques, and Bennett's collection of Indonesian and Guatemalan textiles enrich the spaces.

The home took three years to complete, due to the area's short building season and the care that was taken to leave the site as undisturbed as possible. The house has worked the way it was planned. Bennett now shares the home with Russell Betts, an environmental and international travel consultant. Both enjoy the indoor/outdoor lifestyle and are completing a few more interior projects, as well as restoring the land where a road once ran in front of the original cabin. The grassy courtyard—the space between the bedroom and living wings—is being slowly transformed into an outdoor living room, further blurring the line between indoors and out.

In the meantime, though, there is the meadow to watch, a number of bears to count and the sound of the wind rustling through the pines to hear.

COOPER-HAGGARD RESIDENCE

Tassajara Canyon, California

In 1994, while Polly Cooper and her husband, Ken Haggard, were visiting her father in Little Rock, Arkansas, an arsonist was busy setting fire to a hillside that would burn more than forty thousand acres in Central California. The fire whipped through Tassajara Canyon, where the couple lived, then jumped a freeway and continued on. Haggard and Cooper, both architects, returned home to find a blackened canyon filled with ashes and their house nothing more than molten glass and charcoal. The only two remaining structures were a concrete slab and a stucco-covered straw bale bench.

After recovering from their loss, Haggard and Cooper turned their attention toward rebuilding their home. The survival of the straw bale bench convinced them that a house made from bales would have a chance of enduring another wildfire. They also knew that straw had the benefit of being a good insulator. Cooper and Haggard are partners in a thriving architectural practice specializing in sustainable designs and use of alternative energy sources. Cooper also teaches architecture at California Polytechnic State University in San Luis Obispo, while Haggard mans the office and works with clients.

Although devastating, the fire left many dead trees on Cooper and Haggard's forty-acre parcel, including sycamores, white alders, pines, firs, and cypress. This presented an opportunity to use resources directly from the property by milling and cutting the burned wood into usable lumber. They brought in a portable mill and were surprised at the quantity and quality of wood that was produced.

The first step was to build a small structure that would serve as their temporary headquarters where they could work and live while reconstructing their lives. They decided to use rice straw bales, which are easily obtained in California, and a post-and-beam structural system on the existing slab from an old shed that had burned in the fire. The compact structure contained a kitchen, an eating area, and a living space, plus one bedroom and a bathroom. Haggard and Cooper decided on a free-form style of architecture with undulating walls topped by a green sheet metal roof. This building later became their guest quarters.

Tucking in the straw bales as in-fill on three sides, the architects used frame construction with large windows on the south side to capture the sun's heat. The exterior

Undulating straw bale walls and a multilevel elevation make this an unusual complex with many artistic features.

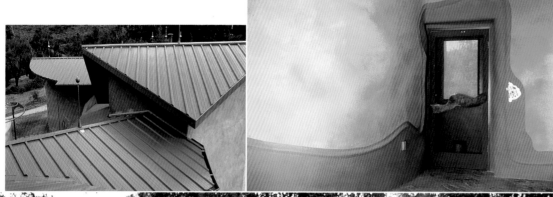

straw bale walls were covered with portland cement stucco; the interior walls with two coats of stucco and a final thin coat of gypsum plaster. Completed in 1995, the small building was built to be off the grid, with both active and passive systems that include photovoltaic cells and a Pelton wheel, a small water turbine that produces hydropower from a creek that bisects the property.

Once the couple completed their temporary headquarters, they began building a 1,200-square-foot, one-story office for their architectural practice that would be linked to a 2,000-square-foot, two-story residence. The three wings of the structure are in a U-shape around a courtyard. There are several entrances to both house and office. Connecting the office in the south wing to the residential side of the complex is a wing that houses a laundry room, a library, and a reading area. Haggard and Cooper put the active part of their residence on the first floor, including a living room, a dining and kitchen area, and a spare bedroom, and kept the more private areas, a master suite and a guest bedroom, on the second floor.

The contemporary structure has many sculptural elements. There is also a surprising combination of green sheet metal roofing and purple flashing and trim, in contrast to the free-form, undulating earthen-pink walls. Small bits of melted glass, more reminders of the 1994 fire, were embedded in the stucco. Chains hang from the end of roof gutters to the ground, enticing rainwater to flow down the metal links. This classic Japanese approach, Haggard says, is a celebration of water in a place that receives little rain.

Since both Haggard and Cooper were happy with the way their first structure turned out, they chose post-and-beam construction once more for their office and main residence, using heavy timbers with straw bales on three sides, stacked on edge to create a slightly slimmer wall than standard straw bale construction. The couple felt this would still provide enough mass to keep interior temperatures stable. The stem walls were formed eight inches above grade, preventing any possible moisture contact. The timbers were so beautiful that Haggard and Cooper decided to wrap the bales around the outside of the post-and-beam structure and leave the interior framing exposed, rather than tuck the bales between the posts.

To meet California's stringent seismic building codes, Cooper and Haggard decided on eight-inch-thick interior masonry partition walls that are also load bearing, have

Opposite, clockwise from top left:

The elevation of the house and office provided an opportunity for an interesting roofline. The sheet metal roof is fire-resistant and easy to maintain.

On the existing slab the fire left behind, the homeowners built a small structure that gave them a place to live and work during the rebuilding of their new home and office. The building is now a guest house.

Ponds remain from when the property was a trout farm. The homeowners, who are architects, designed a post-and-beam structure with a straw bale wrap on the outside, allowing the straw bales to be shaped with curves.

thermal mass, and function as decorative entries between spaces. The bales were reinforced with vertical and horizontal rebar.

The interior details and fine finish work add to the handcrafted feel of the home. The Italian tile flooring used in the kitchen, dining area, and office was inset with shards of colored tiles, mementos found among the ashes from the previous home. The living room has an exposed aggregate floor, a textured surface comprised of small stones and concrete. It was coated with several layers of sealant to give it a lasting sheen. Milled wood from the fire, which shows off the knots and whorls of the trees, was made into windowsills for the kitchen and dining area. A local craftsman fashioned cabinetry in the kitchen and office from white alder burned in the fire. Leading to the second floor is a free-form railing whose undulations and irregularities mirror the home's exterior walls. An old oak barrel is used for the cabinetry in the downstairs bath.

Natural illumination fills the interior rooms. Glass blocks, set above the counters in the kitchen, spread muted light across the work space. Transom windows above interior hallway doors can be left open for cross ventilation. The office is light and airy from a bank of

south windows and clerestories. Both office and residence were designed with south-facing walls made up of a combination of windows, water tank walls, and Trombe walls. The tanks of water absorb sunlight and radiate the heat into the house; Trombe walls are glass-fronted masonry made for maximum solar gain in the winter. The double-glazed, argon-filled windows have heat-receiving, low-emissivity glass and resist heat or cold more than conventional double-glazed windows. The house was designed to cut out direct summer sun with generous roof overhangs. Skylights, providing extra daylighting and heat, can be operated by a special technology. These "skylids," manufactured in Albuquerque by Zome Works, open and close via a thermally activated fluid. Manual controls were also installed. Since summer temperatures in the area can reach 110 degrees Fahrenheit, the office was designed with sixteen-foot-high ceilings and ceiling fans that work in conjunction with operable clerestory windows to vent out hot air. Where bales weren't used for roof insulation, cellulose was blown between the rafters. An attic fan helps with ventilation.

The main house and office are, like the first house, also off the grid. A combination of solar panels provides hot water; twelve panels of photovoltaic cells, electricity; and a Pelton wheel, hydropower. Gauges on a wall near the office allow Haggard and Cooper to monitor how much photovoltaic energy is available and if they need to switch to backup hydropower. It's a way of making them conscientious about their energy consumption. For energy-efficient lighting, Haggard and Cooper chose compact fluorescents throughout. Appliances, including a solar refrigerator, are superefficient. Low-water-use toilets were also installed, and the kitchen stove uses propane.

Just a few years ago, Haggard and Cooper replanted white alders, which are already twenty feet high. Other species of trees continue to regenerate, their seeds growing into young saplings. Most important, they feel they are doing their small part for future generations by practicing conservation and good stewardship.

Opposite, top: Taking their cue from the free-form straw bale walls, the home-owners designed a railing that has a curving bannister at the head of the stairs and cutout metalwork.

Opposite, bottom: Ample daylighting in the kitchen comes from a south-facing window wall and skylights. A ceiling fan and crank windows help circulate the air. Slabs of wood milled on site were used for window ledges and a center countertop.

Above: The pleasant offices were designed with drafting tables placed against the south wall where windows, clerestories, and skylights provide daylighting. The Italian floor tiles have a durable finish and are easy to maintain. The office conference table is made from a sycamore that burned in the 1994 fire.

chapter 4

REINVENTED, RECYCLED, AND HIGH-TECH MATERIALS

PEOPLE HAVE ALWAYS BEEN ENTERPRISING IN FINDING materials to construct homes. Since ancient times, stone, wood, and even brush have been shaped into shelters that respond to their environment. When natural materials weren't readily at hand, builders, even in ancient times, recycled, borrowing from a neighbor's abandoned structure or searching a trash heap for reusable items.

Technological innovations have enabled the manufacture of new materials that are energy efficient and environmentally sound.

The most innovative contemporary use of logs and stone is by builders, architects, and homeowners who work with local materials. This approach not only helps create a home compatible with its environment, but lowers transportation costs and use of fossil fuels. It also supports the local economy.

The popularity of recycled materials is also booming. New businesses specializing in everything from salvaged doors and woodwork to bathtubs and concrete slabs have sprung up around the United States. Even today's standard frame and stucco construction is being rethought to create homes that are efficient and user friendly.

These advances also allow waste to be turned into building materials. One company manufactures blocks from recycled wood chips, a waste product of the wood industry. The blocks, known as Faswell blocks, are combined with a slurry of cement to achieve a higher insulation value than standard concrete. They are also lighter and easier to work with and can be cut with a handsaw. Still other energy-efficient blocks on the market are made with recycled polystyrene. Rastra is one such product; when set into walls it has the added benefit of a high insulative value. Cellulose, another by-product of the wood industry, is popular for insulating homes. When compressed, it can be formed into custom insulating panels for walls and roofs in timber frame construction. The weight of each panel varies, depending on the length between the posts.

Another innovation involves casting lightweight volcanic rock, or pumice, into walls, using enough concrete to bind the rock together. The fourteen-inch-thick honeycomb walls are easy to finish and have an insulative value of R-20 or better. Straw, also a waste product, is the main element in several building materials other than bales. A company in Toronto,

Canada, produces particleboard from chopped straw. The company claims that it is moisture-resistant and easy to work with.

Standard frame and stucco, can be transformed as well. Conscientious architects and builders use strategies such as sensitive siting—placing a home so it responds to the topography, prevailing breezes, and path of the sun—and incorporating efficient energy systems.

A look at the future of building reveals an even wider variety of high-tech solutions. John Picard, a Los Angeles environmental consultant, is a forerunner in the implementation of technology to create networked homes. Picard is experimenting with the construction of his own home. Internet technologies in the house will be able to relay information on water and energy output to Picard and let him and manufacturers know when parts need replacing. Among other functions, his house will anticipate energy needs with a thermostat tied into the National Weather Service. Lights and the security system will be able to be operated from anywhere in the world. The house will be built with nontoxic materials and be energy efficient.

SPRINGDALE FRUIT COMPANY

Springdale, Utah

At Zion National Park in southern Utah, buttes, mesas, and jagged mountains loom high above the canyon floors. Bands of mineral pigments stain the exposed rock walls with colors of the rainbow. Adjacent to the park are two thousand acres bisected by the east and north forks of the Virgin River, and riparian corridors lined with thick stands of cottonwood and salt cedar trees.

The owners of this property asked Virginia-based architect William McDonough to create a working community for the Springdale Fruit Company on a portion of the land, which would include a company store, a packing plant, a pumping station, and houses for staff and owners.

One of the owners is a New York–based businessman and former Harvard professor who had a long-held dream of purchasing land in this remote region for its agricultural potential. In 1983, after two years of searching for the right property, he found this spectacular location, where he began planning an organic produce farm that will eventually have two hundred acres planted in apples, pears, peaches, and other tree fruits. His plan was to leave the majority of the land untouched, its rocky escarpments and long stretches of red earth covered with wildflowers

and high-desert shrubbery contrasting with the pockets of fruit trees planted in neat rows that would follow the topography. The other owner is a friend who believed in the concept enough to help support it financially and occasionally stay at Springdale Fruit Company in the main house that was designed and built for him.

The farm is a work in progress; to date, close to 50 percent of the trees have been planted and 80 percent of the buildings are in place. The overall schematic for the project was a collaborative effort between architect William McDonough and the owners. McDonough, a graduate of Yale's School of Architecture, is known internationally for his "green" approach to commissions. His involvement in environmentally oriented architecture began while working in the Jordan River Valley between undergraduate and graduate school, studying how traditional architectural forms of the Mideast had been adapted to suit the climate and other natural conditions. McDonough applied the same philosophies for the Springdale project; the result is an architecture that responds to its landscape, climate, and history.

The elevation at the Utah farm is 3,900 feet. Winters can be harsh, with cold winds, snow, and sleet. During

Above: The Springdale Fruit Company sits on two thousand acres that abut Zion National Park in southern Utah.

Opposite: In the main house, an assortment of baskets and pottery accents the living area of the great room. The fireplace is used for heat during the winter months. For added warmth, there is radiant floor heating.

July and August, strong winds blow while thunderheads build in preparation for early-evening rains. Moisture that isn't absorbed in the soil runs down the slopes and over the land, feeding the streams and aquifers below. The runoff carries the soils with it, slowly changing the earth's contours. This runoff is collected and used to water the eighty existing acres of orchards planted on the valley floor.

Originally, the property was occupied by Shone, a Paiute chief, but by 1861, a group of Mormon settlers, under the direction of Brigham Young, settled the land and founded the township of Shoneburg. The pioneers, practitioners of polygamy, built homes, planted small orchards, and grew vegetables. They always fought the ebb and flow of their environment, which included yearly flooding from the east fork of the Virgin River. Crops were wiped out, fields dried, the dirt eroded, and the settlers became discouraged. Eventually the residents of Shoneburg moved on, abandoning their homes and other structures.

Oliver DeMille, a leading citizen of the community, was the last of those to leave Shoneburg, in 1896, with his two wives and children. He left behind an architectural legacy—an impressive two-story sandstone house built about 1865 on the rise of a hill. The DeMille house, now

an empty shell, along with the abandoned town homes, became the inspiration for the architectural style of the buildings at the Springdale Fruit Company.

McDonough designed the houses using indigenous materials acquired from local sources. Three homes built for staff members are simple, two-story, passive solar designs that take advantage of their setting. The interiors have wood plank floors, hand-hewn beams, four-panel fir doors.

McDonough refers to the homes by number. Closest to the highway is House One, a double-walled structure with an exterior of sandstone blocks that came from a nearby quarry. Although the interior walls are built from standard concrete masonry block, a layer of insulation in an air space between the two walls keeps inside temperatures stable. The wood shingle roof, a material that mirrors its historical predecessors, has deep overhangs that shelter generous porches on the front and back of the house from the searing midday sun. The surrounding orchard acts as a buffer from the winds, heat, and road noise.

House Two is also double-walled, but with adobelike block on the exterior. These exterior blocks were made nearby from local materials that include volcanic cinders

Opposite, clockwise from top left:

The back patio of the main house has spectacular views of the surrounding landscape.

A porch on the main house shades the entry and can be used as an outdoor room on summer evenings. Antiques are mixed with functional outdoor furniture.

Carefully set into the ridge of a hill, the main house takes advantage of the surrounding views. Large windows directed for optimal passive solar gain incorporate the landscape into the architecture.

or aggregate, sand, and cement with iron oxide for pigmentation. The blocks were tied to standard concrete masonry blocks on the interior, with a layer of insulation in between. The structure is tucked against a south-facing hill that shields it from the north winds and helps insulate it in winter. Tall cottonwood trees just south of the house provide shade in the summer, but lose their leaves in the winter, allowing the sun to heat the walls and penetrate the interior through the windows. Jalapeño chiles, tomatillos, and grapes grow in the garden.

House Three, also double-walled, uses the same pressed adobelike block as House Two on the exterior and standard concrete block on the interior. It, too, is snuggled against a protective hillside.

House Four, or the main house, has a view of the old DeMille home. Whereas the DeMille house is set on the crest of a hill with a rugged mountain backdrop, the main house is next to a hill, with the roofline becoming an extension of the ridgeline, making the house and hill appear as one. Following the contour of the site, McDonough placed the one-story house on a southeast-northwest axis and divided it into three main spaces. The great room, in the center, includes living, dining, and kitchen areas,

spanned by an open-truss ceiling fashioned from local logs. To the west of the great room is a wide corridor that doubles as an office and leads to a master bedroom suite. On the east are two guest bedrooms and a utility room that accesses a basement used for storage and as a wine cellar.

The main house, an evolution of ideas beginning with the area's first settlers, required choosing building materials that were close to the site. Both owner and architect felt that transporting materials long distances involved greater use of fossil fuels, something both of them wanted to avoid. The original DeMille house was built from sandstone blocks that came from a local quarry. McDonough suggested using irregular sandstone blocks, also from a nearby quarry, for the main house, fitting the blocks precisely, similar to those at Machu Picchu in Peru. Like the other Springdale houses, the main house is double-walled with insulation and concrete masonry block on the inside, covered with gypsum plaster.

Each part of the main house has a relationship with its surroundings, through a window or a door, enticing the occupants to explore the environment beyond. In the great room, a large floor-to-ceiling window faces north, capturing the sweeping vistas of hills, valleys, and

Opposite, clockwise from
top left:

The homeowners chose
comfortable furniture
upholstered in heavy cotton
for the conversation area.

Marble countertops are used
in the kitchen of the main
house. The large center
island is for food preparation
as well as for serving. The
stonework of the back wall
matches the exterior.

A large window in the
master bedroom of the main
house connects the interior
to the outside. The antique
furnishings help tie the
house to the area's history.

Right: The southern Utah
soil and climate support
trees that produce healthy
crops of sweet, organic
apples.

sculpted mesas. In the master bedroom, a huge arched window frames panoramic views. The master bath has ties to the outdoors through a large picture window that is directly in front of the tub.

On the west end of the great room, a fireplace serves as a focal point in the center of an intricately faced sandstone wall. The east kitchen wall is also faced in sandstone. Alder, an indigenous wood from Utah, was chosen for the cabinetry and paneling. Fir, also native to Utah, was used for the plank flooring. A center island divides the food preparation area from the living area.

Architect and owner agreed on a pitched roof with copper gutters and drains to shed moisture easily. The three primary sections of the roof, covering the master suite, public space, and guest bedrooms, are wood shingle, and the two connecting areas, office and laundry, are covered in sheet metal. Deep overhangs shade the entry and create an exterior living room that receives only late-afternoon sun in the summer and full sun in the winter. Screens on windows and doors allow the house to be left open for ventilation. A thick stand of junipers, planted on the southwest side, blocks wind and intense summer sun. Instead of a garage, which would disrupt the integration

of land and architecture, there is only a parking area partially dug into a hillside. The north side of the home has an open, sandstone-paved patio that looks out over a vast panorama of dramatic landforms with the DeMille home featured prominently in the foreground.

Furnishings in the main house have a Southwestern flavor, with Native American baskets and bowls and Navajo rugs. In the master bedroom, a four-poster bed is covered with an old quilt, and an armoire sits in one corner. Antique chests of drawers are used in all the bedrooms, along with kerosene lanterns. Books, many about the area's landscape, flora and fauna, and history, line built-in shelves in the office, hallway, and living room. McDonough also designed the packing plant and store to conform with the rest of the architecture, matching the block used for the exterior walls at Houses Two and Three.

Owners and architect, working together, chose a vernacular architecture rooted in local history, which celebrates the breathtaking scenery while showing respect for the environment. Springdale, a working farm, is a well-planned enterprise that has only minimal impact on the land, using only 10 percent for development and leaving 90 percent as natural habitat.

CHOUINARD RESIDENCE

Central California Coast

Walls exposed to the elements have a layer of insulation. Air Krete, a nontoxic, cementious foam insulation, was blown into a cavity created by fasteners attached to the wall and window screening. The insulated wall was then finished with traditional lath and plaster. Recycled slabs were used for walls and walkways as well as steps.

Mountains form a rain shadow to the north of the house. The house was sited to protect it from cold onshore winds.

Enticed by good surf and the proximity to water, Malinda and Yvon Chouinard purchased property on the Central California coast and planned to build a simple encampment—a shelter that would have minimal impact on the environment. They originally envisioned a lockable garage space where they could camp and store belongings. But the possibility of large gatherings of family and friends convinced the couple to expand the plan to include a communal living space and bedroom wings.

Longtime environmental activists, the Chouinards initially felt that having a second home conflicted with their philosophy that no one should have more than a single small, energy-efficient residence. They ameliorated what they called their "feelings of guilt and hypocrisy" by deciding to construct their retreat from local trash. Their original intent was to reuse materials such as rubble from buildings destroyed by California's recent earthquake. The Chouinards hired Santa Ynez–based architect Robert Mehl and contractor Kit Boise-Cossart to come up with a plan and materials for the retreat. Unable to find a source for earthquake rubble, the architect and contractor instead came up with a plan to build the one-story, 1,400-square-foot home with regionally available recycled wood, salvaged roof tiles, chunks of discarded sidewalk, and torn-up slabs from demolished buildings. The home's power is supplied mainly by the sun.

The property, with its rolling grassland, coastal cliffs, and ocean views, provided a spectacular building site. The owners, together with the architect and builder, chose a site that would shelter the home from the onshore winds. Tucked behind a rise in the land, with one side opening to the Pacific Ocean, the house is barely visible from the road. Access is on a driveway consisting of recycled road base from a local demolition company.

Entry is on the northeast, shielded from the winds by the topography, as well as a freestanding garage and one wing of the house. An informal foyer opens into a great room with a kitchen and a dining area at one end, a living area and a loft at the other. A guest bedroom and bath and a master suite flank the great room.

Exterior and interior walls were finished with a mixture of textures and colors. Smooth, amber-colored plaster walls contrast with exposed aggregate blocks formed from concrete rubble. A wood shingle roof with wide overhangs and a deep porch to the rear are similar in style to a European cottage. A low garden wall skirts the periphery.

Walls of concrete rubble and pavers create a patio around the outside of the house.

Below: Patio walls
curve to form an
enclosed garden area.

The challenge for Robert Mehl and Kit Boise-Cossart was finding building materials to fit their clients' parameters. The search entailed juggling aesthetics, cost, and product availability. Boise-Cossart found a demolition company that agreed to supply concrete taken from old dairy barns and broken sidewalks. These salvaged pieces were sculpted on the site into rough-finished blocks using only sledgehammers and masonry chisels. The blocks were then used to build massive exterior and interior house walls, garden walls, and pathways. Using the chiseled concrete slabs fit the style envisioned by the Chouinards, who were inspired by the stone architecture they had seen during visits to the Iberian Peninsula.

Before laying the walls, Boise-Cossart and Mehl went to Chaco Canyon, in New Mexico, to study the masonry work of the Anasazi. The trip proved inspirational. They decided to leave the walls of the Chouinard house exposed where they were protected by the roof overhangs, patterning them after the ancient rock work at the archaeological site. Other walls, open to the elements, needed an additional layer of material to make them more energy efficient. Extensive research led to a product called Air Krete, a nontoxic cementitious foam insulation. Adhering the foam

to the recycled concrete blocks took some ingenuity. Boise-Cossart devised a system to attach to the outside block fasteners that would protrude several inches. Window screening was hooked to the fasteners, creating a cavity where the Air Krete could be blown in. Traditional lath and plaster were used to finish the exterior walls.

The garage walls were built like those for the house. The large roof timbers were recycled from an old pier in Ventura, California. Because some of the wood was infested with termites, the building team used a chemical-free approach to eliminate the pests. A long, deep pit was dug and lined with plastic, then filled with water, where the wood soaked until it was free of termites. Other posts and beams were cleaned by spraying or brushing with a borate salt solution.

Part of the original plan was to build a fireplace for the great room that would function as a bearing wall, but when the Chouinards decided to scrap it, another roof system needed to be devised. Yvon Chouinard came up with the solution. He forged metal tie rods that spanned the width of the room, creating an open truss roof system.

Roof tiles were recycled from a liquor store that was being demolished. Lumber for the roofing and trusses was

the product of old forest fires in the Central California area. The owners opted for solid wooden shutters on the exterior, which were milled from a salvaged redwood bridge near Ojai, California. The shutters not only screen out light, but also help to stabilize interior temperatures.

Recycled materials were found for many interior details. Reject wood from the Gibson Guitar Company, curly and bird's-eye maple, was used by craftsman Gary Bulla to build a chopping block. The country-style cabinetry was crafted by Bulla, from local woods. Almost all the hardware was scrounged by Bulla from garage sales, swap meets, and junk shops. The wood front for the solar refrigerator was inspired by a model illustrated in an old Sears catalog, giving the appliance the look of handcrafted furniture. The kitchen's fine woodwork provides a pleasing contrast to the rough, exposed walls. The flooring and bathroom countertops were salvaged from the trash piles of local building sites, then laid and grouted in irregular shapes.

The Chouinards chose other environmental strategies. Water for the house is stored in a round holding tank next to the garage. Seven solar panels heat the domestic hot water and supply radiant floor heat in every room. The Chouinards never need to turn on the floor heat; the

massive walls keep interior temperatures stable year-round. If the water/heat system is in high demand, a flash hot-water heater kicks in and supplies extra energy. A woodstove is used in the living area. Photovoltaic cells supply energy for most of the electricity, but a conventional power source is available for rare lengthy periods of cloudy weather.

In keeping with the Chouinard's original intention to build a simple dwelling, the interior furnishings are sparse—a few chairs, a wooden table, several shelves filled with books. Upholstered pieces in the great room make inviting spots to curl up and relax.

The garden and patios were outlined with dry-stacked masonry walls made from chiseled concrete slabs. Vegetables and flowers fill planting beds along the walkways. Prayer flags add color to the gardens near the house. New trees were planted along the drive. The Chouinards left the rest of their property natural, with native grasses and low-growing scrub.

The Chouinards' home is their sanctuary, not meant to impress anyone. They come here to enjoy the sound of waves pounding against the shoreline and feel the breezes from the Pacific Ocean. And of course, Yvon Chouinard is here to surf.

Above, left: The kitchen cabinetry was built from a mix of recycled woods by a local craftsman. The flooring was made from broken pieces of roofing slate that were recycled from builders' trash piles.

Above, right: Utilitarian furnishings fit the homeowners' goal for a house that needs little attention or maintenance. French doors off the master bedroom open onto the south patio. The room has strong cross ventilation in the summer when the doors and windows are open.

Opposite: The great room opens onto a covered porch that screens the room from the summer sun. Window shutters can be closed during the day to keep the room from overheating or at night to prevent heat from escaping. Furnishings are eclectic and comfortable.

TWO WEEKEND RETREATS

San Antonio, Texas

David Lake and Ted Flato started their San Antonio–based architectural firm in 1984 with a desire to create buildings shaped by local climate and geography, and to use materials and systems that work well with the environment. Two weekend retreats in the San Antonio area designed for two separate families exemplify their innovative approach. One is a lakeside house that uses orientation and building strategies to make it environmentally friendly; the other is a minimal encampment near a creek.

A two-lane blacktop road skirts the periphery of a small lakeside community north of San Antonio, Texas, where the first of these weekend retreats is located. Thick stands of oak and cedar are mixed in with splashes of wildflowers and grassy meadows. Although summers can bring uncomfortably high temperatures and high humidity, breezes from the south and southwest offer some relief. Three months out of the year, during the height of the winter, frigid winds whip across the plains and down through central Texas. This is Texas Hill Country, home of Lyndon B. Johnson. The Alamo, Mission Francisco de la Espada, Mission San Jose, and numerous other monuments all testify to a region that

has attracted diverse cultural groups over the centuries.

David Lake, Ted Flato, and John Grable, principals of Lake Flato Architects, spearheaded the design of this lakeside retreat. They came up with a simple 1,200-square-foot floor plan with enough space to accommodate their clients, a young family of three, and friends. The style is a hip-roof home patterned after Texas farm buildings with ventilators on top.

The location is on a lake at the end of a dirt lane that branches off the main road. A mailbox and an unpaved parking area are the only signs that a home is tucked into the trees below, sheltered and screened from view. A gentle hill and concrete steps lead down through the front yard and up to the main entrance of the house.

A long narrow lot and a small budget made this a challenging project for the Lake Flato team. The architects put the public areas on the first floor and placed sleeping spaces on the periphery of both floors: two on the bottom with one bath and three, plus a second bath, on the second story.

To the north, or facing the road, the house is burrowed into the slope, protecting it from the harsh winter winds. Entry is through single-pane French doors that open

The Lake House's rear view reveals a much different elevation, showing the full two-story height of the home, which is carefully sited among the native trees. The inspiration for the architecture came from rural farm buildings in Texas.

Right: The kitchen, with its vintage refrigerator and stove, is set into an alcove on the first level. The homeowners, who are active water enthusiasts, chose concrete flooring and utilitarian furnishings for easy maintenance. The lake-side doors are thirteen feet high on the south side of the house. They let in direct light and heat during the winter, making the house a year-round getaway.

Opposite, top to bottom:

Old-fashioned fixtures are used in the upstairs bathroom.

Narrow stairways that flank the entry landing lead up to sleeping areas and the bathroom.

onto a concrete landing. A grand stairway leads down to the first level, or main living space, bringing an unexpected change in elevation. The main living space reaches twenty-five feet high and culminates in a cupola.

The central core of the house, which architect John Grable calls the "universe," consists of the entry, a living-dining-kitchen area, and a tall, shallow screened porch overlooking the lake. An alcove at one end of the main floor houses a Rumford fireplace, a big, shallow fireplace designed to throw heat into the room. An alcove at the opposite end has an efficient kitchen. When the south doors are open to the screened porch, the entire room opens to the outside.

Although the walls are made of frame and stucco, the architects used an innovative approach to creating a thermally comfortable interior. Small bedrooms, bathrooms, and a storage space, tucked into the outer corners of both the first and second floors, make up what the architects call an outer insulating envelope. These rooms, as well as six-inch walls filled with conventional insulation, act as a buffer between the outside cold or heat and the central core. The cupola has electronically controlled glass windows that vent out hot air and capture cool breezes, creating what the architects call a "chimney effect." The front entry doors line up

with the glass doors on the opposite side of the house to provide cross ventilation. Windows aligned with interior barn doors provide maximum ventilation for the central living space and help cool the entire volume. In winter, the sun penetrates the glass on the south doors and heats the concrete floors. Strategically planted trees help shade the outside walls. All these features ensure that the house maintains a stable year-round temperature. Only during rare periods of extreme heat or cold is backup heating or cooling necessary.

Furnishings are utilitarian. A long wooden refectory table seats eight. The entry stairs function as a seating area during large gatherings, an idea borrowed by the architects from New York brownstones. An upholstered love seat and chair provide comfortable seating in the living area, and an old chest serves as a coffee table. The kitchen's focal point is a vintage stove and refrigerator. Baskets, scattered throughout the house, are stuffed with reading materials and toys.

For the second weekend retreat, the clients wanted a shelter that "if left unattended would disappear into the landscape within one hundred years." The family of four, who enjoy hiking and bird-watching, envisioned an elaborate lean-to, or *jacal*, that would protect them from the elements, but still offer a close relationship with nature. *Jacal*

Top, left: Native cedar logs support the shed roof. The limestone walls act as a shield, sheltering the interior from harsh winter winds while providing storage space for future solar equipment.

Bottom, left: For the retreat's dining table, the homeowners chose pigskin furniture from Mexico, which is comfortable and ages well.

is a Spanish word that refers to a shed or simple structure. In Texas, the *jacal* was the first building erected on a ranch for use until more substantial buildings could be finished.

Located forty-five minutes from San Antonio, the clients' acreage, which is bisected by a running creek, lies on limestone bedrock embedded with fossils. Wild turkeys nest in the tall grasses, and deer graze among the lush growth of juniper, oak, black walnut, and big tooth maple. Bird life is abundant in the spring; the air is often filled with the song of the canyon wren. Ted Flato spent time walking around the property, discovering where the land opens up to the summer breezes and where it is sheltered from winter winds. Both architect and clients agreed the house should be located on a rocky ledge not far from a creek, where the sound of running water was still audible.

Inspired by the sleeping porches of old vacation homes, Flato created a simple thousand-square-foot floor plan—basically a large room with screening on three sides and a sleeping and kitchen alcove sheltered by a north limestone wall. "You don't go to the country to go into four walls," Flato told his clients when describing his design.

The curving limestone wall, which shields occupants from cold northern winds, has German mortar joints, a

building technique indigenous to this region. Located along the wall are sleeping and cooking alcoves and a Rumford fireplace. Above the wall is wood framing with galvanized sheet metal flaps and screening. The flaps can be opened with a rope and pulley for cross ventilation in the summer and closed for maximum protection in the winter. Open gable ends on the east and west sides invite sun in winter. The clients wanted a "no-maintenance" shelter, so Flato chose for the main area decklike wooden flooring that has been sanded and oiled and is easy to keep clean. The floors in the alcoves and service rooms are concrete slabs. Cedar logs from the site were used to construct the building's simple post-and-beam system, finished off with the screening and a shed roof. Deep overhangs to the south create a porch.

In the kitchen alcove, fence piping supports the wood plank shelving, and galvanized sheet metal covers the counter. Above the sink, a small square window cut into the limestone wall lets in muted north light. The sleeping alcove is a cavernous space with two small windows and enough room for a bunk bed and dresser. Tucked into the west end of the limestone wall is the only bathroom, an outdoor facility with a composting toilet and a simple showerhead. Old cedar fence posts from the site span the top of the bathroom walls to form a ceiling that is open to the sky.

There is no electricity. Light is provided by kerosene lamps, candlelight, and flashlights. The refrigerator uses propane, the composting toilet peat moss. Rainwater harvested in a cistern is brought to the house by a photovoltaic-powered pump. A solar panel heats the water.

As the weather turns cool, the family moves the furniture closer to the fireplace in the main room. There the parents sleep in an antique iron double bed on wheels. Meals are served on a Mexican pigskin table and chairs. A couch and an old chest that doubles as a coffee table sit in the middle of the room most of the year. Built-in limestone shelves, part of the fireplace wall, hold books, games, and lanterns.

The owners talk about how their screened *jacal* sings in the wind and the sounds it makes as rain hits the corrugated sheet-metal roof. This is the place where they relax away from the city and find pleasure in small things: the fossils they unearth next to their shelter; the birds that nest in the rafters; and the striking insect, a walkingstick, that clings to the screen door.

Above, left: Enclosed by screening and protected by a back wall of curving limestone, the retreat is more akin to an elaborate camp. Deep overhangs on the south side provide plenty of shade. Ventilation flaps above the limestone wall on the north side can be closed as protection against cold, winter winds. Furnishings are easily moved around the room as seasons change.

Above, right: A galvanized tub is used for washing up and shaving. The water is harvested rainfall from the roof. On the other side of the limestone wall is a bathroom with a composting toilet and an outdoor shower.

HUNT RESIDENCE

Napa, California

When Phyllis Hunt purchased an eight-acre hillside lot in Napa, California, in the early 1990s, she knew instinctively she couldn't build just any house on the site. She wanted something organic and welcoming, something that fit the land. Her instincts proved her quite right—in more ways than one.

Though always privately owned, the oak-covered hill sat in the middle of one of Napa's oldest neighborhoods, and local residents had been using the hill for generations as a park. They picnicked, hiked, and practiced rock climbing on the boulders at the top of the hillside. From below, some even worked on their golf swings—old golf balls dot the lower reaches of the slope. Deer and other wildlife roamed between trees and boulders. Before Hunt's purchase, neighbors and city officials had defeated five previous home proposals for the site.

Hunt, a health-care professional, wasn't daunted. She felt she could offer the neighborhood a home that was pleasing and inviting, not, as she puts it, "a tract house on steroids." More important, she was willing to keep the land open to neighbors, as it had been in the past.

As Hunt pondered her piece of the hillside, her thoughts centered upon a round shape for the house, something

Below and opposite: Low rock walls embrace the house, which curves into its hillside setting. The windows capture the sun's warmth by day and provide views of city lights in the evening.

A native rock table is a quiet spot for contemplation in a patio carved out in the hillside behind the house.

A resident feline marks time on the living room's solar calendar.

The influence of Frank Lloyd Wright's circular houses is most evident in the exterior curves of the house and the low roof overhang. The rock retaining wall follows the hillside; the path leads toward the front of the house.

that was nestlike and nurturing, yet took advantage of the views of the valley below. She asked Berkeley architect Craig Henritzy to design the house. She had seen one of his previous designs, a home with rounded forms, and thought he could interpret her ideas.

Henritzy brought several significant ideas to the design process. Having studied the architecture and culture of California's indigenous people, he suggested a Native American motif for Hunt's house, creating, in effect, a solar observatory on the hill. Henritzy also steered Hunt toward choosing an environmentally friendly building material for the home's walls, Rastra elements, a precast forming system of long modules made of recycled polystyrene and cement.

As Henritzy walked the land with Hunt, they discovered a faint deer path that wound through a spot where they planned to set the house. Using the path as the inspiration for the spine of the plan, the architect designed a half-circle form for one side of the spine, the back of the house, snugged into the hillside, and half of an ellipse for the front, which overlooks the city below. Henritzy divided the 2,400-square-foot house into four levels to take advantage of the slope. Private areas—the

three bedrooms and two baths—were placed in back, at the highest level, toward the hill. Entry, kitchen, and dining room are in the middle; the living room is at a lower level, facing Napa. The lowest level is a small storage area, tucked beneath the kitchen.

Once the plan was in place, the home's architectural style began to evolve. Henritzy melded Frank Lloyd Wright's organic principle of allowing the site to influence a building's design with features inspired by ancient ceremonial round houses that native tribes had built in the region. The home rises majestically from its site, yet blends into the hillside. Neighbors and local planning officials approved the design.

Before construction could begin, however, Hunt and Henritzy hit an unexpected snag. Soil tests revealed a huge, crumbling boulder in the middle of the site where they had wanted to position the house. Water percolated through the decomposing rock, which had to be removed.

Once the building pad was cleared and construction commenced, the logic behind Henritzy's choice of material became clear. Rastra, developed in Europe in 1968, is recycled polystyrene—the material found in fast-food and disposable coolers—mixed with cement

The home's levels correspond with the slope of the site. In the Pueblo-Revival living room, the scored concrete floor also includes a solar calendar, which is progressively illuminated until the winter solstice.

and shaped into hollow forms. The forms are lightweight and easy to cut into rounded shapes with a tool as low-tech as a handsaw. Building Rastra walls can be done by unskilled labor. Shaping Hunt's rounded walls, therefore, proved to be simple and quick; the Rastra was a better choice for the design than other, less maneuverable materials.

To build Hunt's walls, the Rastra elements were stacked vertically atop a stem wall. Plumbing and electrical lines were set into the hollow cavities of the elements, then the cavities were filled with concrete. The walls, once set, are virtually fireproof and are said to have an insulative value up to R38.

To conform to the area's seismic codes, reinforcing steel was placed in the wall system's cavities, before the concrete was poured. The exterior was covered in a golden-colored stucco; the interior walls were hand-troweled with a mottled ivory-hued plaster.

The placement of the windows was important. Not only were they meant to provide views and light, but their exact location created a solar observatory within the house. As a bonus, the windows also worked with the passive solar strategies for the home.

To get the windows just right, the architect visited the property often to observe the sun's path and the shadows created on the building site, then used a computer to calculate the sun's exact position throughout a calendar year. Inspired by native tribes' primitive calendars, Henritzy designed a solar calendar and had it scored into the center of the living room's concrete floor. As the weeks pass, triangle markers carved into the floor are illuminated by sunlight. At solar noon on December 21, the winter solstice, for instance, the entire length of the calendar—and all of the triangles—are illuminated. Small windows were placed at the sides of the house to capture the rays of the sun during each solstice and equinox. At those times of the year, sunlight from the windows falls on sculptural markers set between columns in the house.

During winter months, when the sun is at a low angle, it warms the scored concrete floor and the mass of Rastra walls. In summer, the windows are shaded by roof overhangs and by a metal trellis designed by local sculptor Robert Ellison. Operable skylights throughout the house vent out excess heat.

The interior was inspired by Pueblo Revival homes of

Opposite: Openings from upper-level bedrooms overlook the kitchen, designed around a 1920s range that the homeowner brought from her previous residence. Floors throughout the house are acid-stained concrete.

Right, top: A mesh and metal panel provides a design element outside the powder room door.

Right, bottom: Beams are attached to the lodgepole pine columns with sculptural brackets.

the 1920s and the 1930s. The ivory-plastered Rastra elements were shaped into ziggurat staircase enclosures and fireplaces. The concrete flooring—typical of Pueblo Revival homes—was updated by staining it with acid to achieve colors ranging from red and rust to pale greens. Lodgepole pine columns in the center of the house emphasize the open volume. Interior ironwork by sculptor Ellison reiterates the home's sinuous design. The shape of the metal sconces was taken from the floor plan.

The open plan and sculptural backdrop allow Hunt to display an eclectic collection of furnishings and accessories that include antiques, family treasures, contemporary pieces, tapestries, and art photography. The effect is comfortable and inviting—there are many places to curl up with a good book or spend time engaged in conversation.

Hunt has been working with a local artist, Gary Miller, to create a series of patios, delineated by native rock walls, that wrap around the entire perimeter of the house. Miller incorporated some of Hunt's broken crockery into the rock walls, as well as old golf balls found during construction. The largest patio, off the living room, makes a comfortable spot to entertain and watch hot-air balloons rise from the distant vineyards. A

slightly smaller patio is tucked behind the master suite. Hunt has planted raised beds with herbs and flowers close to the home, while the rest of the hillside has remained in its natural state.

As the house neared completion, it was named Napacha, with *cha* roughly translating as "community house." The house warming included a blessing by a California Pomo Indian, a ceremony that connected Napa-cha with its design philosophy.

Since then, Hunt has had numerous gatherings of friends and family. Guests circulate naturally from the front door through the kitchen and down past the dining room, unknowingly following the old deer path. The first year she was in the house, Hunt hosted a winter solstice party on December 21. Just as planned, a beam of light shot through its designated window and hit its intended mark.

BIBLIOGRAPHY

BOOKS

Alexander, Christopher; Ishikawa, Sara; and Silverstein, Murray. *A Pattern Language.* New York: Oxford University Press, 1977.

Baars, Donald L. *The Colorado Plateau.* Albuquerque: University of New Mexico Press, 1983.

Boyle, Bernard Michael. *Materials in the Architecture of Arizona, 1870–1920.* Tempe: Architecture Foundation of the College of Architecture, Arizona State University, 1976.

Burba, Nora, and Panich, Paula. *The Desert Southwest.* New York: Bantam Books, 1987.

Clark, K., and Paylore, P. *Desert Housing.* Tucson: University of Arizona Office of Arid Lands Studies, 1980.

Corbishley, Mike. *The World of Architectural Wonders.* New York: Peter Bedrick Books, 1996.

Cuming, Harry and Mary. *More of Yesterday's Tucson Today.* Tucson: West Press, 1996.

de Blij, Harm. *Harm de Blij's Geography Book.* New York: John Wiley & Sons, 1995.

Easton, David. *The Rammed Earth House.* White River Junction, Vt.: Chelsea Green Publishing Company, 1996.

Fathy, Hassan. *Architecture for the Poor.* Chicago: University of Chicago Press, 1973.

———. *Vernacular Architecture.* Chicago: University of Chicago Press, 1986.

Fisher, Leonard Everett. *Great Wall of China.* New York: Macmillan Publishing Company, 1986.

Hannaford, D., and Edwards, R. *Spanish Colonial or Adobe Architecture of California, 1800–1850.* Stamford, Conn.: Architectural Book Publishing Company, 1990.

Heede, Richard. *Homemade Money.* Snowmass, Colo.: Rocky Mountain Institute, 1995.

Iowa, Jerome. *Ageless Adobe.* Santa Fe: Sunstone Press, 1985.

Jacobson, Max; Silverstein, Murray; and Winslow, Barbara. *The Good House.* Newton, Conn.: Taunton Press, 1990.

King, Bruce. *Buildings of Earth and Straw.* Sausalito, Calif.: Ecological Design Press, 1996.

LaPorte, Robert. *Moose Prints: A Holistic Home Building Guide.* Fairfield, Iowa: Natural House Building Center, 1993.

McHenry, Paul Graham, Jr. *Adobe and Rammed Earth Buildings.* New York: John Wiley & Sons, 1984.

Moore, Suzi. *Under the Sun.* Boston: Bulfinch Press, 1995.

Newcomb, Rexford. *Spanish-Colonial Architecture in the United States.* New York: Dover Publications, 1990.

O'Connor, John F. *The Adobe Book.* Santa Fe: Ancient City Press, 1973.

Pourade, Richard F. *The California to Remember.* San Diego: Copley Books, 1979.

Sheridan, Thomas. *Los Tucsonenses.* Tucson: University of Arizona Press, 1997.

Steen, Athena Swentzell; Steen, Bill; Bainbridge, David; and Eisenberg, David. *The Straw Bale House.* White River Junction, Vt.: Chelsea Green Publishing Company, 1994.

Trimble, Marshall. *Roadside History of Arizona.* Missoula, Mont.: Mountain Press Publishing Company, 1986.

Weir, Bill, and Blake, Robert. *Arizona Traveler's Handbook.* Chico, Calif.: Moon Publications, 1996.

World Book Encyclopedia of Science, "Earthquakes," *The Planet Earth,* 1991.

PERIODICALS

Bennett, Noel; Wakeman, Jim; and McGuire, Michael. "A Place in the Wild," *Environmental and Architectural Phenomenology Newsletter,* 1991.

Brown, Patricia Leigh. "Houses the Cows Would Love to Eat," *New York Times,* 12 December 1991, section C1.

Bruning, Nancy. "A Down-to-Earth Home," *Garbage,* June/July 1993: 15–16.

Buturian, Linda. "Beyond the Bale," *Utne Reader,* September/October 1997: 76–78.

Calmenson, Diane Wintroub. "Healing the Environment with Bricks and Byte," *Interiors & Sources,* October 1995: 29–35.

Dagostino, Paul. "Alternative Building Materials," *Phoenix Home & Garden,* May 1998: 34, 36, 38–39.

Davidson, John. "Simone Swan Adores Adobe," *Historic Preservation,* March/April 1999: 52–59, 104, 114.

Easton, David. "Rammed Earth Homebuilding," *Mother Earth News,* April/May 1996: 34–43.

Environmental Building News Editors. "Project: The Chouinard House," *Environmental Building News,* January 1999: 12–13.

Everett, George. "Straw Homes," *Mother Earth News,* October/November 1993: 54–58.

Fatsis, Stefan. "Earth Homes: Building Mansions of Soil," *Wall Street Journal,* 20 September 1996, section B10.

Frazier, Deborah. "Utes Turn to Mountain for Refuge: Tribe Protects the Warrior They Believe Protects Them," *Rocky Mountain News,* 19 September 1994, section 6A.

Gannett, Alison. "Colorado: Crested Butte High Baling," *The Last Straw,* Winter 1998, Issue 21: 25–26.

Haggard, K., and Cooper, P. "Rising from the Ashes: A Study in Sustainability," *Solar Today,* September/October 1998: 26–30.

Hamm, Keith. "Back to the Land," *The Independent,* 15 May 1997; 23–28.

Horrigan, Alice. "Affordable by Design," *E. Magazine,* July/August 1997: 28–34.

King, Bruce. "Straw-Bale Construction," *Building Standards,* September/October 1998: 18–24.

Klinkenborg, Verlyn. "Pioneer Aesthetic for Utah: A Stone House Inspired by the Land and Its History," *Architectural Digest,* October 1995: 134–141, 227.

Kunzig, Robert. "A Tale of Two Archaeologists," *Discover,* May 1999: 84–92.

Lund, Laurel. "The Last Straw," *Natural Home,* May/June 1999: 46–55.

———. "Down to Earth Design," *Natural Home,* September/October 1999: 38–49.

McDonough, William. "The Next Industrial Revolution," *Atlantic Monthly,* October 1998: 82–89.

McLeister, Dan. "Straw-Bale Construction Gaining More Acceptance," *Professional Builder,* September 1996: 70.

Metropolitan Home Editors. "The Jorgensen, Rancho Redux: Adobe Sets the Stage," *Metropolitan Home,* November 1986: 96–101, 119.

Miller, Lauraine. "Homes from the Earth," *Houston Chronicle Magazine,* 12 July 1998; 6–9, 14, 16–18.

Osborne, Sally Eauclaire. "Building with Straw," *Home,* May 1995: 56–60.

Rosenblatt, Roger. "William McDonough: The Man Who Wants Buildings to Love Kids," *Time,* 2 February 1999: 70–73.

Steen, Athena, and Steen, Bill. "Building with Straw Bales," *Mother Earth News,* December 1995/January 1996: 40–49.

Talarico, Wendy. "The Nature of Green Architecture," *Architectural Record,* April 1998: 149–152.

Tibbets, Joe M. "Rammed Earth: Developing New Guidelines for an Old Material," *Building Standards,* September/October 1998: 8–11, 16.

Wagner, Michael. "Home Eco-nomics," *Metropolitan Home,* November/December 1996: 66–67, 75.

Weisman, Alan. "The Eco-Wizard," *Los Angeles Times Magazine,* 11 January 1998: 16–19, 34.

Wendel, Kelly. "Rammed Earth Gives New Meaning to Dirty House," *Phoenix Business Journal,* 18 October 1996: 30.

Whiteley, Peter O. "Building Tomorrow's Home," *Sunset,* May 1998: 192–196.

WEB SITES

Durtschi, Al. "An Introduction to the Navajo Culture," www.waltonfeed.net/peoples/navajo/culture.html

Earth Island Journal. www.earthisland.org

Focus Multimedia. "Catalhoyuk Architecture (ancient adobe city)," www.focusmm.com.au/~focus/civcty/cathyk04.htm

Lowenhaupt, Harris. "Cast Earth: A Breakthrough Technology in Light Construction." www.castearth.com

Steen, Bill and Athena. "The Straw Bale Earthen House," www.deatech.com

RESOURCES

GREENLEE RESIDENCE

Builder
Todd Swanson
Bio-Hab Adobe Homes
Durango, CO
(970) 259-5985

Cabinetry
Thurston Kitchen and Bath
Boulder, CO
(303) 449-4001
www.thurstonkitchenandbath.com

SMITH RESIDENCE

Architect
Elizabeth Wagner
Santa Fe, NM
(505) 988-4020

Interior Design
Jane Smith
Jane Smith Interiors
Basalt, CO
(970) 927-4660

Landscape Architecture
Faith Okuma
Design Workshop, Inc.
Santa Fe, NM
(505) 982-8399
www.designworkshop.com

**Cabinetry, Shutters, and
    Specialty Furniture**
John Oliver
Santa Fe, NM
(505) 471-1702

Chandelier
Crystal Farm Antler Chandeliers
    and Furniture
Redstone, CO
(970) 963-2350
www.crystalfarm.com

JORGENSEN RESIDENCE

Builders and Designers
Richard Jorgensen and
    Charlotte Lykes Jorgensen
Sugarloaf Building Company, Inc.
Boulder, CO
(303) 444-1742

Landscape Design
Azure Canyon company
Boulder, CO
(303) 938-1163

ADOBES DE LA TIERRA

Builder
John Mecham
Earth & Sun Adobe
Scottsdale, AZ
(602) 329-9994

Landscape Architecture
Phil Hebets
Sonoran Desert Designs
Cave Creek, AZ
(480) 595-6400
www.sonorandesertdesigns.com

WIGGINS-LOGAN RESIDENCE

Architect
Jim Logan Architects PC
Boulder, CO
(303) 449-3274
http://jlogan.com

Adobe Blocks
Richard Levine
New Mexico Earth
Alameda, NM
(505) 898-1271

Pigments, Sealers, Stains, and Finishes
BioShield Paint Company
(505) 438-3448

Pigments, Stains, Sealers, and Thinners
Livos Naturals
Pine Plains, NY
(800) 343-6394 or (518) 398-9663
www.livos.com

LINGS-FERGUSON RESIDENCE

...hitect
...Logan Architects PC
...der, CO
...) 449-3274
...://jlogan.com

...der
...on Davis
...wood, CO
...) 327-4451

...be Blocks
...Anderson
...Desert Adobe
...tewater, CO
...) 626-5253
...v.newmexicoearth.com

...inetry
...Coniglio
...wood, CO
...) 596-1744

...erior Doors and Custom Windows
...Sibley
...der, CO
...) 494-6093

...t Materials
...Country Gardens
...a Fe, NM
...) 925-9387
...v.highcountrygardens.com

...r
...a Orzel
...t Solar Works
...) 626-5253
...v.solarwork.com

...AN RESIDENCE

...igner and Builder
...n Group
...idio, TX
...) 277-4425
...v.adobealliance.org

...IGHT-EASTON RESIDENCE

...der
...id Easton
...med Earth Works
...a, CA
...) 224-2532
...v.rammedearthworks.com

...hitect
...e Baushke
...artus
...Francisco, CA
...v.apparatus.com

...den Consultant
...mas Nemcik
...n, CA
...) 224-0646

Recycled Beams and Lumber
C & K Salvage
Oakland, CA
(510) 569-2070

Sconces
Jeff Reed
Reed Studio
Oakland, CA
(510) 261-9888

BARRIO NEIGHBORHOOD

Designer and Builder
Tom Wuelpern
Rammed Earth Development, Inc.
Tucson, AZ
(602) 623-2784
www.rammedearth.com

Vigas and Saguaro Ribs for Ceilings
Old Pueblo Adobe
Tucson, AZ
(520) 744-9268
www.oldpuebloadobe.com

Antique Mexican Doors
Galleria San Ysidro
El Paso, TX
(915) 544-4444
www.galeriasanysidro.com

McGEE RESIDENCE

Architect and Builder
Paula Baker Laporte, AIA
Eco Nest Building Co.
Tesuque, NM
(505) 984-2928
www.econest.com

Straw-Clay Workshops
Robert Laporte
Eco Nest Building Co.
Tesuque, NM
(505) 984-2928
www.econest.com

INDOOR/OUTDOOR RESIDENCE

Architect and Builder
Paul Weiner
DesignBuild Collaborative
Tucson, AZ
(520) 792-0873
www.dbcarchitectbuilder.com

Rammed Earth Contractor
Quentin Branch
Rammed Earth Solar Homes, Inc.
Oracle, AZ
(520) 896-3393
www.rammedearthhomes.com

Concrete Flooring
Carson Concrete Specialities, Inc.
Tucson, AZ
(520) 325-0557
www.carsonconcrete.com

Concrete Fireplace and Stem Walls
Benchmark Concrete
Tucson, AZ
(520) 293-1305
www.benchmarkconcrete.com

LOW RESIDENCE

Architect
Edward Jones
Jones Studio, Inc.
Phoenix, AZ
(602) 264-2941
www.jonesstudioinc.com

Rammed Earth Contractor
Quentin Branch
Rammed Earth Solar Homes, Inc.
Oracle, AZ
(520) 896-3393
www.rammedearthhomes.com

General Contractor
Sigma Contracting
Scottsdale, AZ
(602) 788-7800
www.sigmacontracting.com

Cabinetry
Meyer and Lundahl Manufacturing Company
Phoenix, AZ 85009
(602) 254-9286
www.meyerandlundahl.com

Silver-Leafing
Randy McCabe
Laveen, AZ
(602) 237-4199

HARDING RESIDENCE

Architect
Paul Weiner
DesignBuild Collaborative
Tucson, AZ
(520) 792-0873
www.dbcarchitectbuilder.com

Builder and Custom Tile Work
John Woodin
Woodin Construction
Tucson, AZ
(520) 327-3282

Cabinetry
Paul Heald
Alamo Woodworkers Collective
Tucson, AZ
(520) 882-9490

Living Room Sofa
Arroyo Design
Tucson, AZ
(520) 884-1012
www.arroyo-design.com

GANNETT RESIDENCE

Designer and Builder
Alison Gannett
Crested Butte, CO
(970) 349-2021
www.alisongannett.com

Roof Panel Systems and Natural Wood Finishes
Eco-Builders, Inc.
Crested Butte, CO
(970) 349-0525

WARKENTIN RESIDENCE

Designer and Project Architect
David Arkin, AIA
Arkin-Tilt Architects
Berkeley, CA
(510) 528-9830
www.arkintilt.com

Principal Architect
Sim van der Ryn
Inverness, CA
(415) 669-7005

Builder
Paul Aurell
Gray Construction
San Anselmo, CA
(415) 457-8661

Ryegrass Ceiling Panels
Meadowood Industries
Albany, OR
(541) 259-1303
www.meadowoodindustries.com

Recycled Trusses and Siding
Recycled Lumberworks
Bellingham,WA
(303) 243-0781
www.oldwoodguy.co,

Recycled Doors
Urban Ore
Berkeley, CA
(510) 841-7283
www.urbanore.citysearch.com

BENNETT RESIDENCE

Architect
Michael McGuire
Stillwater, MN
(651) 439-3710

Art Work
Noel Bennett
(505) 989-9988
www.noelbennett.com

COOPER-HAGGARD RESIDENCE

Architects
Ken Haggard and Polly Cooper
San Luis Obispo Sustainability Group
Santa Margarita, CA
(805) 438-4452
www.slosustainability.com

Solar Products
Zomeworks Corporation
Albuquerque, NM
(800) 279-6342
www.zomeworks.com

SPRINGDALE FRUIT COMPANY

Architect
William McDonough, FAIA
William McDonough + Partners
Charlottesville, VA
(434) 979-1111
www.mcdonough.com

CHOUINARD RESIDENCE

Architect
Robert Mehl
R.P.M. Architects
Santa Ynez, CA
(805) 688-7281
www.gballiance.com/rpmehl.html.com

Builder
Kit Boise-Cossart
Gaviota, CA
(805) 567-1400
www.kbc-gbs.com

Cabinetry
Gary Bulla's Architectural Woodworks
Santa Paula, CA
(805) 933-1366
www.garybulla.com/aw

Appliances
Sun Frost
Arcata, CA
(707) 822-9095
www.sunfrost.com

Alternative Power Products
Schott
(800) 777-6609
www.us.schott.com/english.com

Composting Toilet
Sun Mar Composting Toilets
Tonawanda, NY
(416) 332-1314
www.sun-mar.com

TWO WEEKEND RETREATS

Architects
David Lake, FAIA
Ted Flato, FAIA
John Grable, AIA
Lake Flato Architects, Inc.
San Antonio, TX
(210) 227-3335
www.lakeflato.com

Water Collection System and Solar Pum
Richard Heinichen
Tank Town
Dripping Springs, TX
(512) 894-0861

Composting Toilet
Sun Mar Composting Toilets
Tonawanda, NY
(416) 332-1314
www.sun-mar.com

Propane Refrigerator
Temptrol Corporation
San Antonio, TX
(210) 341-6239

HUNT RESIDENCE

Architect
Craig Henritzy
Indigenous Designs
Berkeley, CA
(510) 526-8601
www.henritzy.com

Rastra Elements
InteGrid Building Systems
Berkeley, CA
(510) 845-1100
www.integrid.com

Landscape and Wall Design
Gary Miller
Jessell Gallery
Napa, CA
(707) 257-2350
www.jessellgallery.com

Sconces, Custom Steel Work, and Sculpture
Robert W. Ellison
Penngrove, CA 94951
(707) 795-9775
www.robertellison.com

DITIONAL SOURCES

hitects and Builders

bara Dietz-Ballantyne, Architect
couver BC, Canada
4) 730-0312
w bale

ert E. Barnes, Architect
son, AZ
0) 744-9268
w.oldpuebloadobe.com
be

hael Frerking
ng Systems Architecture
w.michaelfrerking.com/
cializing in cast earth

n D. Kelly, AIA
ta Barbara, CA
5) 963-1013
w.jdkaia.com
tainable design

n D. Kelly, AIA
ta Barbara, CA
5) 963-1013
w.jdkaia.com
tainable design

Donough Braungart Design Chemistry
rlottesville, VA
4) 295-1111
w.mbdc.com
motes eco-friendly design prinicples and
ports cradle-to-cradle product manufacturing

dscape Design

belle Green & Associates
ta Barbara, CA
5) 569-4045
w.gballiance.com/isabellegreene.html
toxic straw particleboard

ducts

Greene
ttsdale, AZ
0) 946-9600
w.akagreene.com
-friendly building products

-Products, Inc.
lder, CO
w.ecoproducts.com

ensage.com
Francisco, CA
5) 453-4915
w.greensage.com
ectory for sustainable building & furnishing
ducts; member of the U.S. Green Building
ncil

bord Enterprises, Inc.
tland, OR
3) 242-7345
w.isobord.com
ntoxic straw particle board

Natural Territory
Scottsdale, AZ
(480) 998-2700
www.naturalterritory.com
*Green furniture, organic home textiles, and
earth-friendly paints*

Real Goods Trading Company
www.gaiam.com/realgoods/
*Eco-friendly building products, products for
solar living*

Trex
www.trex.com
*Recycled composite decking from plastic bags and
waste wood*

Organizations

Biotique Habitat
Constructionfibres.free.fr/home.html
Consultation on straw bale construction

California Straw Building Association (CASBA)
Pacifica, CA
(805) 546-4274
Promotes the practice of straw building

Rocky Mountain Institute
1739 Snowmass Creek Rd.
Snowmass, CO 81654
(970) 927-3851

The Canelo Project
Tucson, AZ
(520) 455-5548
www.caneloproject.com
Straw bale workshops, design, and consultation

Development Center for Appropriate
  Technology (DCAT)
Tucson, AZ
www.dcat.net
*Straw bale workshops and consulting; rammed
earth and adobe construction*

Ecological Building Network
San Rafael, CA
(415) 987-7271
www.ecobuildnetwork.org
Information on sustainable architects and builders

Institute for Sustainable Design
School of Architecture, Campbell Mall
University of Virginia
Charlottesville, VA
(804) 924-6454
*Interdisciplinary approach to sustainability
research*

Second Nature, Inc.
Boston, MA
(617) 224-1610
www.secondnature.org
*Consultants to universities and colleges on
sustainability education*

Rocky Mountain Institute
Snowmass, CO
(970) 927-3851
www.rmi.org
*Think tank dedicated to environmental
stewardship*

U.S. Green Building Council
Washington, DC 20036
(202) 828-7422
www.usgbd.org
*Information on building green, including LEED
(Leadership in Energy and Environmental
Design), the nationally accepted benchmark for
green buildings and their rating system*

Reading

*Cradle to Cradle: Remaking the Way We
  Make THings*
By W. McDonough & M. Braungart

Environmental Building News—
  Building Green, Inc.
www.buildinggreen.com

Fractal Architecture: Design for Sustainability
By Ken Haggard and Polly Cooper

Inter-Americas Adobe Builder Magazine
www.adobebuilder.com

The Last Straw Journal
www.strawhomes.com

Natural Building Network (NBN)
www.naturalbuildingnetwork.org

Natural Home Magazine
www.naturalhome.com

Solar Energy International
www.solarenergy.org

A Sourcebook for Green and Sustainable Building
www.greenbuilder.com/sourcebook

Information

Cellulose Insulation Manufacturers
  Association (CIMA)
Dayton, OH
(937) 222-2462

Energy Star
www.energystar.gov
Labels and promotes energy-efficient products

Forest Stewardship Council
www.fscus.org
*Promotes certified wood harvested from well-
managed forests*

Natural Resources Defense Council
www.nrdc.org
Information on environmental and social issues

[Resources] **201**

ACKNOWLEDGMENTS

IN PUTTING TOGETHER A BOOK SUCH AS THIS, IT WAS our intent to showcase a variety of homes representing the different architectural forms, approaches, and styles of adobe, rammed earth, straw bale, and other alternative materials. Along the way, we received help, information, and encouragement from many individuals.

First and foremost, we thank the homeowners, architects, builders, and designers whose houses we have featured in this book. With patience, understanding, enthusiasm, and humor, they let us into their homes and their lives. Without them, there would not have been a book.

For their special talents, support, and leads, we extend our gratitude to Dan Budnik, Mary Burba, Madelaine Cassidy of Pentax, Tanya Chan of E2, Sheldon Coleman, Chris and Lisa Conyers, Burke Denman, Denver AIA, Barbara Dietz-Ballantynne, Nolan Doesken, Joann Dornan and Michael Dunn, Michael Frerking, Penny Gibbs, Gillie, Bruce Glenn, Lynn Greene, Todd Grissett, Richard Grossman, Richard Heede and Alexis Karoleides of the Rocky Mountain Institute, Steve and Joan Kent, Julia Kerfot, Christy Lee, Mary Ellen Long, Melanie Lunsford, Brian Madden, Carol Martin, John Oliver, Lee Pardee, Kevin Paul, Lisa Peacock, Chiara Roll, Margaret Sanders, Shakespeare, Paul Shoenfield, Linette Shorr, Judith and Randy Udall, John Willet, Denise and Mark Wills. Thanks also go to Peter Whitely of *Sunset*, Manya Winsted of *The Santa Fean*, Laurel Lund of *Natural Home*, and Laura Hull of *Metropolitan Home*.

Special thanks go to William McDonough, Athena and Bill Steen, David Bainbridge, David Eisenberg, Ken Haggard and Polly Cooper, Jim Logan, Hunter and Amory Lovins, John Picard, Matts Myhrman and Judy Knox, David Easton and Cynthia Wright, Robert Barnes, Quentin Branch, Bill Tull, John Mecham, and others who have pioneered the way.

To our editors and designers at Chronicle Books, we would like to thank Leslie Jonath, Jodi Davis, and Julia Flagg.

INDEX